D1164757

UNDER THE TREE OF LIFE

The Religion of a Feminist Christian

Gail Ramshaw

Continuum • New York

1999

The Continuum Publishing Company
370 Lexington Avenue
New York, NY 10017

Copyright © 1998 by Gail Ramshaw

Printed in the United States of America

Library of Congress Cataloging-in-Publication Data

Ramshaw, Gail, 1947–
    Under the tree of life : the religion of a feminist Christian /
Gail Ramshaw.
        p.   cm.
    Includes bibliographical references.
    ISBN 0-8264-1110-X
    1. Feminist tecology.   2. Feminism—Religious aspects—
Christianity.   I. Title.
BR83.55.R36 1998
261.8′344—dc21   98-27845
                                                                      CIP

Contents

An Introduction

To begin, let me cite a passage from Virginia Woolf's *The Years*:

> She always wanted to know about Christianity—how it began; what it meant, originally. God is love, The kingdom of Heaven is within us, sayings like that she thought, turning over the pages, what did they mean? The actual words were very beautiful. But who said them—when? Then the spout of the teakettle puffed steam at her and she moved it away. The wind was rattling the windows in the back room; it was bending the little bushes; they still had no leaves on them. It was what a man said under a fig tree, on a hill, she thought. And then another man wrote it down. But suppose that what that man says is just as false as what this man—she touched the press cuttings with her spoon—says about Digby? And here am I, she thought, looking at the china in the Dutch cabinet, in this drawing-room, getting a little spark from what someone said all those years ago—here it comes (the china was changing from blue to livid) skipping over all those mountains, all those seas. She found her place and began to read.[1]

For twenty-five years Virginia Woolf has been in my mind. Reading her novels in graduate school, I wanted to become a writer. When at age thirty-five I moved with my family to a larger apartment that had a study, granting me once again a room of my own, I took up her inquiry: will women write differently from men? A picture of her hangs in my office now, the only wholly secular image in the room. For despite this one character in this one novel, Woolf herself evidenced no interest in religion, no curiosity about what "the kingdom of Heaven" meant. It was not Christianity that sparked her.

Now I recognize in this passage of Woolf's an outline of my life's work. For it is I who always wanted to know about Christianity. I have written book after book about what its beautiful words and images mean. I have studied in seminary to know which men wrote what about which other men. I have wrestled, as have countless educated Christians, with whether what the men wrote was false or true. And in the company of many feminists I must face the question of whether women care to value what men wrote about men. Unlike Woolf, I do feel the Christian spark, but I must think about it.

This book records my engagement with that spark. It alternately energizes and shocks me, enlightens and burns me, that spark skipping over the seas.

Let me first account for why I care about religion at all.

It is safe to assume that everyone reading this book is to some degree religious. Some part of our memory, our values, our daily or annual rituals originated in religion or echoes religious patterns of life. For the Hasidic Jew, that religious patterning is life-encompassing. For the American secular humanist, it is negligible, only faintly back on the screen at funerals or Christmas time. I am a person with lots of religion. Religion was in the story of my widowed immigrant great-great-grandmother seeking free education for her sons and finding it at a Lutheran school; it was there in my parents' commitment to give more money each year to the church than to the Internal Revenue Service; my education was church-sponsored, my friends are involved with religion, my career is religiously oriented. And I have no desire to amputate that considerable part of myself. Indeed, I want rather to embrace it more fully, to be more wholesomely contained by it. And I believe that the psyche of many people would be healthier were they to pay more attention to their religious part, whether it is still well attached or nearly fallen off.

Another comment in defense of religion. I was raised under the post-war fantasy that within a few decades nearly everyone in the world would look and act and think like Americans. They'd all come to accept Christianity, to vote for Democrats, and to practice rights for women. But this patronizing view of how to achieve world peace has been stunned by observing the unfurling of a new tribalism for which each hitherto no-account group has hoisted a tattered flag found in some attic corner. All over the globe, folk are reaffirming ancient myths and reviving traditional rituals. Even to understand the daily newspapers we must learn about archaic religions, newly alive and energizing activist communities. Perhaps, then, it is time also for Christians to reaffirm their ancient myths and revive their traditional rituals. At least this woman is passionate to discover which myths and rituals still have some breath in them. We need not club our neighbors over the head with our communion ware, but we can honor a chalice used by our people for centuries and can commission an artist to craft a new one that draws us all toward its round circle of shared life.

Next, some definitions, so that you will know what I'm talking about.

In first world countries, the word "religion" has more and more come to mean one's personal beliefs, perhaps even opinions, about life, liberty, and the pursuit of happiness. Perhaps since the Reformation, certainly since the Enlightenment, it is the "I" of each self that can choose to what degree to engage in a religious life. Many people assume that religion is solely about the I. Although most of my college students have been reared in the church and have studied Roman Catholicism continuously throughout their elementary and secondary education, they are also individualist Americans, children of Ralph Waldo Emerson, and many of their comments in class discussion evidence the worldview that truth is relative and that there is no authority with the right to tell them what to believe. Bookstores are filled with accounts of spiritual journeys which have mostly to do with the spirit of the self. Since it is nearly impossible for the lone individual to formulate and maintain a coherent and meaningful philosophy and ethic, religion these days is like the contents of people's bedroom closets: markedly individual, rather private, more or less disorganized, and usually short-lived.

In teaching religion in college, I have found useful a traditional definition of religion as a communal worldview about ultimate reality with requisite rituals and ensuing ethics. Religion is not, I suggest, about a Hallmark-card angel, sent to say hello; it's about ultimate reality, community, ritual, and ethics. Yes, in our culture in which the self-reflective consciousness is nurtured perhaps beyond its worth, the individual must, yes, decide daily and weekly and annually how much to participate in religious activities. But I find conversation clearer if we proceed with some definition of religion beyond personal biography. A woman told me that she is a Jewish Quaker witch who strongly identifies with the Virgin Mary, and she asked me what I thought of something-or-other. What I thought was, this woman has no religion.

Thus, in the first place, I admit to Knot Number One: I want religion to be the way the tribe lives because of how the tribe believes. I want religion to be the profound, even stunning, manner in which the community celebrates its ideas. But I cannot fool myself. Having lived in seven different states, traveled across the seas, completed three graduate degrees, married twice and, for thirty years, studied the brilliancies, the abominations, and the nonsense in Christianity and other world religions, I am no tribal member. I am not able to tread along peacefully in the footsteps of my dead relatives. I want an unwieldy marriage: I want intelligently to affirm a set of communal beliefs. I want freely to elect the rituals and ethics of a community. I do not know if I want the impossible.

The religion in question is Christianity. The word "Christian" is not easy to define. By this word some people refer only to those who have memorized the same catechism and who belong to the same clubs; others use the word as a synonym for "nice." Let me propose that to be Christian is to ritualize the resurrection of Jesus Christ and to embody the Spirit of God in the world. It is not that all Christians agree on what "the resurrection of Jesus Christ" was and is, or how best to "embody the Spirit of God," but that if there is no way that this language has meaning for you, you are not Christian. The road is wide, but there are curbs on both sides.

But here is Knot Number Two. Yes, Virginia Woolf, how do we know whether the words are true? What man did what when, and which men wrote it down, and why? Since it was hoped by the writers that their words could describe a world beyond our world, a vision farther than our seeing, a level deeper than language, how much of the sacred text must, by necessity, be metaphor? We can all agree with Thomas Aquinas that "God is Rock" is metaphor. But what about "the kingdom of heaven," or "the resurrection of Jesus Christ"? Indeed, what about the word "God" itself? The mystic Meister Eckhart urged us beyond the metaphor "God." Were the fourteenth-century churchmen correct when they judged Eckhart a heretic? Had he replaced God with only the play of his own mind? Or is the term "God" best understood as a metaphor for noble aspirations, and are Sunday mornings better spent building houses with Habitat for Humanity? We could word this second query in this way: how much of Christianity is life-altering reality, and how much mind-pleasing, or stomach-churning, metaphor?

Now a third definition, and the knot it presents.

I am sad that some students find "feminism" a pejorative term. One student stood close to my desk after class and whispered, are you a feminist? Others judge feminism outdated, a movement over and done with. Ha. I define feminism, as do current dictionaries, as the worldview positing equality between women and men and, in consequence, the activism required to inaugurate this worldview. There are male and female feminists, and by no means are all women feminists. Some feminists say that equality must come despite the chasm separating the two disparate, even antagonistic, sexes. Others claim that men, women, and those between are pretty much the same, and so should be treated thus. There's a good deal that feminists do not agree upon.

But feminists who speak American English do agree about the paradigmatic androcentrist word "man." That the noun denoting men can in some contexts include women indicates the male control of definition and category that we reject. We Christian feminists have had to proceed further with our linguistic inquiry, considering one androcentric term after another. Is "father" an acceptable metaphor for God? Is "kingship" an appropriate term for divine status? Is Jesus a viable vehicle for a woman's religious engagement?

Some Christians—I think of the Amish women stitching those stunning quilts—are not feminist. Other believers go further, declaiming that it is not possible for Christians to be feminist, that women's rights are a sin. And it is true that many a feminist, newly convinced that all this Jesus-talk is man-made metaphor that can no longer be nurturing to her, dances out or drifts away from the church. Yet others maintain that feminism is supported by biblical faith. Indeed, the historian Gerda Lerner demonstrates how, in many instances throughout European history, feminist consciousness was birthed in and nurtured by Christianity, the church for example providing an option to marriage and teaching women to read. So it is that many feminist Christians—some enraged, others radiant, settling in on a new branch of the old tree—are writing book after book about the Bible, Christian doctrine, and church life, reshaping old ways with an authority they claim to have derived from God. The third thread, feminism, presents me with Knot Number Three: As a student wrote at the conclusion of her final exam, "P.S. Dr. Ramshaw, how can a feminist be part of Christianity and still hold her beliefs? Thank you, Molly."

This book is about how one woman wants to be and stay both. I want to be both the Cartesian I and a willing member of a ritual and ethical community. I want to be both a skillful archeologist of metaphor and a believer. I want to be both a feminist and a Christian. Either option is an easier place to reside than in the turbulent middle. There is not yet a clear current down the center of the river. I see both banks, but where I am is in the rapids. I have written other books in which I describe feminist Christianity as a wholesome ride on a sturdy ark. Yes, I tell Molly, you can be both. In this book I admit that you'd better wear a life jacket and hold on to a friend. And, who knows: perhaps like Katharine Hepburn on the African Queen, you'll not only slough off the leeches, but you'll get to blow up the enemy ship.

It is as if I want peacefully to sew away at my quilt, twelve stitches to the inch, a prizewinner, but my thread keeps getting knotted. Perhaps I should leave the quilts to the Amish. Instead, I'll remember my great aunt, whose honorable biblical name Hulda was replaced by the nickname Deak when she became a deaconess. She escaped from Lake Wobegon, where she was born and raised, to live in New York City and to drive me around the country on vacations in the 1950s. I named her Chevy IsaBelaire, and we stopped each midmorning for a sweet roll, and I saw how many confections got served under that name. I visited her in a nursing home after her strokes. She was just body parts on a bed, hardly a human there, and I held her hand, knotted and useless, and said over and over, Deak, I'm Gail, Ruth's Gail, do you remember all our car trips? But decades before, when her hands were nimble, she had taught me to embroider French knots. You twist and turn your thread just right, constructing your pattern and forming designs of beauty by careful attention to your knots.

Finally, some words about my title.

Our culture is newly entranced by trees. Some of the women who have fled the churches are gathering at the full moon under great trees, finding only in natural trees a metaphor for life. And our society, having chopped down far too many, now prints trees everywhere. Advertisers use a mythic tree to tempt us into purchasing stationery and sofa pillows and health insurance. Have you seen in that classy catalog the Frank Lloyd Wright tree-of-life silk tie? Raised a Lutheran, and a Lutheran to my core, I was taught to center my faith on Christ's cross—all those years of catechesis, hours of hymn-singing, thousands of sermons, untold Sundays, parochial school devotions, midweek Lenten services, youth group retreats, daily college chapel, worship conferences, all cross cross cross. But as an adult, even I looked up and saw a tree. Indeed, the New Testament calls the cross the tree. In visiting historic churches, I have seen trees everywhere: the fire in a burning tree calling out to Moses, Jonah grabbing onto a tree to pull himself out of the fish's mouth, Christ nailed to a bountifully fruitful tree, the saints surrounding heaven's tree at the end of time. So I must inquire: is my tree of life the copper birch or the pointed fir between my summertime desk and the sea? or the evergreen we encircle with gratitude before we chop it down at Christmas time? or the redbud newly planted in our front yard which I hope will live longer than did our blighted dogwood? Granted, it is the magnificent multi-fruited tree of life that so many religions know as the primary symbol of divine bounty. Can it also be the cross, itself transformed, transforming me, itself needing yet more transformation?

I have decided to write these essays, not because I imagine my thoughts to be somehow unique, but rather because I assume that thousands of people will find my situation familiar. "Always be ready to make your defense to anyone who demands from you an account for the hope that is in you," says one of the most misogynist books in the Bible. So, without pretending to present a systematic theology, I add my Apologia to the pile. We countless feminist Christians need each other. Let's crowd together as our ark heads down the river toward God's sea. Together we'll salute the boats we pass. Did you see the banner on that one?! "In this sign conquer, No feminists allowed." We smile and wave. Together we'll say a sad farewell when a friend abandons ship and swims for the left shore. Together we'll sing some old hymns and learn a few new ones. We hope that if the weather is rotten, at least the wood of the ship is not.

But enough of this water image. I easily get seasick. In the art gallery of the university where I teach hangs a startling anonymous seventeenth-century Dutch painting. Under the massive overhanging branch of a mature tree, surrounded by dozens of the creatures of creation, is Eve blessing the animals. Alone she sits, God's light behind and around her, her naked protruding belly suggesting fertility, as does the rabbit by her feet. Her right hand is upraised and her two fingers extended in the clerical gesture of benediction. Let's join her there with the animals under the tree of life as I work out my description of feminist Christian religion.

Religion is a
communal worldview . . .

I, now fifty years old

As children none of us six brothers and sisters had kiddie birthday parties. My parents judged them, like trick-or-treating and television, to be beneath us. Rather, as I told my first grade teacher to her considerable confusion, my birthday was usually the second Sunday of January, since that was when my godparents could drive up from New York City to Connecticut for a family celebration. Indeed, when I think of kiddie parties, I recall Johnny Steinbeck's birthday, and my pinning-the-tail-on-the-donkey so far off the donkey-chart that all the kids laughed at me.

Even for my fiftieth I did not have a birthday party, although dear friends toasted me at dinners the weeks before and after. Yet I was amazed on my fiftieth birthday, surprised to find myself alive, for I am a perpetual fantasizer of death, my own and that of my loved ones. Since I always assumed I'd be dead by now, perhaps a car crash or ovarian cancer, each day from now on is gift. Thus it was, in part, my turning fifty that impelled me to write these essays, as if after surviving all my imagined deaths I needed to account for my continuing existence.

But I know that many women are writing about their personal experience, whether religious or not, as if in this postmodern time we can speak of nothing but ourselves. We cannot write authoritatively of history, we are told, for it was recorded wrong, and we have only tainted samples to examine. We ought not write theology or philosophy, some women say, for these disciplines are constructs of the oppressor class, men's mausoleums. And since I and many other women are not novelists, we write about ourselves—pretending that a coherent record of our memories and reflections is not itself a novel, an imagined narrative giving sense to one damn day after another.

But as I write these essays, I recall the warning of Carl Jung[2]: we have no right to write about the "innermost life of others." So much for all memoirs filled with tattling about ex-husbands and lousy parents. But what about Jung's warning of "the impossibility of self-portrayal," his judgment that autobiographies are marked by "self-deception and downright lies"? If I ought not speak of others' private life, and I misspeak my own, what is there to write? I think of Mary Daly's recent work describing her "preconception" decision to be born a female. I am not sure how this is different from Samuel Beckett's one-hundred-eleven-page paragraph recording a man's voice babbling from inside a jar. I wonder, on my quietly jubilant fiftieth birthday, what is the value of the lone voice, whether comic or tragic?

The delight in hearing one's own voice is lethal to religion. Religion used to be, and still is for some, a communal worldview about ultimate reality, with the resultant communal rituals and ethics. In most earlier societies, all the people who lived in the same locale endured the same natural disasters, survived the same plagues. And so they buried their dead the same way, they lived by a common code of morality, they sought the same divine assistance and praised the same divine benevolence. Religion was plural. Religion was the way the people lived and, perhaps, thought. But little by little there is evidence of the "I" breaking free from the "we." Are the handprints that surround the prehistoric cave paintings of mammoths personal signatures? How do we account for Augustine's self-analysis centuries ahead of others? In the twelfth-century tale of Christina of Markyate, the spirited story of a woman who, choosing to remain a virgin, even hid herself between the bed curtains and the wall to escape her husband's attack, I am amazed to read the line, "What, I ask you, were her feelings at that moment?"[3] The remarkable narrator urges us to forget the social context within which Christine was expected to marry and to consider, instead, her interior self. The focus on the I sharpens the self, blurs the group, loses the background.

The implications for Christianity are immense. Feminist Christians are only one of many voices now saying that the old group was wrong, blind, that I and my few friends now see. The possibilities for endless fragmentation are rife. At a liturgy conference, the women studying the church calendar are in one group, the women reforming it in another, and in a third room are the women who judge a common calendar hierarchical oppression. The groups get smaller. I gain my I, we lose our we.

About some things I do not miss the we. I still avoid cocktail parties. I have no regrets that I had no kiddie birthday parties, and even after considerable reflection, I say that on Halloween my brother and I had more fun giving out and eating Milky Way bars than I would have had walking up and down Wilcox Avenue getting corn candy and Cracker Jacks, since who really likes corn candy and Cracker Jacks anyway? But I know that religion is finally not about the I. It is about the we before, during and after my I. It is about all that is other beyond my

I. It is about my indispensable, as well as moral, relationship with what is outside me. If there is nothing greater than the self, nothing higher, nothing deeper, nothing divine, no community, we are of all creatures most to be pitied, having a mind to reach beyond ourselves, but with no beyond there to be reached.

So, if I am passionate about certain goods and certain evils in my religious tradition, and I spend my life effecting changes, how do I keep my self from taking over the picture? As I pray evening prayer with my family, and come across the address "Lord," even in the new prayerbook, do I change it? When I go to church, I must decide whether to join heartily in that old cornball hymn with the mushy tune because like "My Darlin' Clementine" it's fun to sing, or whether to go on strike and say, No, not one more time, not those disgusting male chauvinist words. What is the relative value of honoring an historic text versus delighting in words true to my heart? Tradition keeps some things and throws others out. I want to keep more than the I, but I wish no longer to offend the I with the nonsense, or indeed the rot, of a dying we. And when I've made my daily decisions, can I trust the few who praise me? How do I hear those who condemn me?

So in book after book, conference after conference, I say, This is what I hope we keep. I imagine that either extreme is easier: I am I, or we are we. But to affirm that I am we, that we are I: that is tricky, and it is religion in the current time.

Thus, a birthday card to myself: quoting a writer whom scholars refer to as Second Isaiah, a Hebrew poet of perhaps 540 B.C.E., I say,

> *For you shall go out in joy*
> *and be led back in peace,*
> *and all the trees of the field shall clap their hands.*

On my birthday night, wearing a silk dress bought for one-third its price and donning my new birthday jewelry from Mexico, I went out to dine with my husband. The waiters being trained to ignore our conversation, we prayed over our food, in gratitude for present joy, in hope for peace now and peace at the end. I listened for the trees' applause. And I tried to remember, even on my big day, that in Hebrew the "you" is plural.

a feminist, minimizer style

Icame to feminism not in angry reaction against my rearing but as the natural development of my life.

My sister and I agree: The four boys in our family were given no precedence over us two girls. Both boys and girls were expected to excel; both participated in intellectual conversation over the dinner table; both shared the chores of washing and drying the dishes. My parents made it clear that I would be the smartest in my class and might often be smarter than my teacher, female or male. Already in the 1950s my father had jumped over a few decades by hiring a professional woman, whom the company then gleefully displayed at all photo opportunities. My dad's countercultural valuing of a woman's worth at the office corresponds with my daily experience growing up. I never had the sense there was something I was not allowed to do.

I can recall only one single event that contradicted this pattern. Once, in the kitchen, my mother told me that the husband's will must always rule. Perhaps the reason this memory stuck is that, like moving day for the three year old, children remember the disruptive event, the occurrence that didn't fit, the hurricane shaking the treehouse. I remember a sense of puzzlement at my mother's remark, undoubtedly because what I had experienced in my home was not male dominance but, as in most marriages, a complex interplay of whose will prevailed in which situation.

Even in the world of religion, I remember no message of discrimination. Although the church of my childhood ordained only men, in the congregational politics endlessly discussed by my parents, the clergy were often noted for their mediocrity, criticized for their incompetence. My father did not suffer fools gladly, and sometimes the fool was the pastor. On the other hand, the parochial school principal was a highly articulate woman who taught the upper grades and played organ on Sundays and had her own apartment and traveled during the summer months. I had no reason to bemoan my sex, since the religious career open only to males was not one to desire. My mother had brought to my childhood a never-ceasing supply of prairie Protestantism in which the woman with her Bible did just fine, thank you, when the clergyman was out of town.

The androcentrism hit me in college. I observed that although all the male faculty had finished their doctorates, the female faculty had not. I heard perhaps for the first time—had I ignored such a message before?—that men had priority because Adam had been created first. This struck me as a novel and silly idea, and I told the professor that if the male was higher than the animals, because created later, then the female was highest of all, because created last. And when the same professor advised me upon college graduation that I had no future in the field of liturgical language since I was a woman, I recall the interview, just as I remember my mother's remark in the kitchen, because the message was manifestly incongruous; for as a college senior I had already submitted an essay and a prayer for publication.

Undoubtedly some feminists will accuse me of pathological denial, suggesting that their memories of perpetual discrimination are more valid than are mine of equal and respectful treatment. To such a charge I can think of no defense, although I can ask them, as they value women's voices, to receive mine. Some feminists urge women into incessant rage at past and present misogyny. But I am no longer shocked by, and surely take no personal offense at, the alien nature of other human minds or their androcentric cultural patterns. And while I assume that burying patriarchy will take many decades—the pit must be very deep, the corpse is so immense, we keep finding amputated body parts here and there—let me assure you that I know of the unceasing misuse and degrading treatment that most women throughout the world, dead and alive, have experienced. I know the old pattern of buying and selling brides as if they were kitchen utensils and the current practice of advertising half of what we buy as if the purchase includes sex with a beautiful woman. I know of female fetuses aborted, girls sidelined, women forced, burdened by pregnancies, dying in childbirth, slapped around by arrogant males who cite God's law as their warrant. I know the now more subtle ways that women are imprisoned in their anatomy, their freedoms curtailed, their minds overlooked, their values ignored, their contributions marginalized. And I know that since apart from these restrictive lives women were offered nothing, many a woman smiled as she accepted this meager existence. Surely this alone explains how women could go into depression at menopause.

Thinking as a feminist, however, did not mean that I knew how to live like one. I baked bread every Saturday for a long time before it dawned on me that I could write my thesis without kneading dough between paragraphs. It took me a decade of marriage to reclaim my birth name. But categorical condemnations of males or of the church are not true to my life. Indeed, I came into professional competence at precisely the moment that church committees of consequence sought women, and there I was, the youngest person in the boat, pulling my oar along with the men.

Thus, I read Aristotle, not as a patient analyzing childhood agonies, but as an archeologist coming to a dig, fascinated to excavate ruined monasteries and their latrines. My studies have taught me to spot evidence everywhere, everywhere, of the Western pattern of seeing an essential distinction between women and men and of the concomitant practice of ranking the male superior to the female. I saw how this essentialist difference provided the foundation upon which biology, psychology, philosophy, ethics, and religion had constructed their androcentric fortresses. I realized how this mindset had at least tried to keep women closed off in a small corner room, as if we were all Julians, walled up next to the Norwich church, silently observing the liturgy, our visions ignored for the next five hundred years.

Aristotle's biology was, of course, wrong: the male does not supply all that is meaningfully human in procreation; the female is not a passive flower pot, lying quietly underneath, silently nurturing a man's seed. But although the last centuries have shelved Aristotle's biology, studies continue to probe sexual difference. I read that when a woman's estrogen level is high, she has a hard time finding her car in a parking lot. I read about the small difference between the average female brain and the average male brain, the author continuously restating, however, that any particular woman or any particular man may not evidence this gender tendency. It is as if many people believe in Aristotle's essential difference, but are not sure how it is constituted.

During the 1970s I met regularly with other women, seeking communal identity, analyzing sexual oppression. What in the past had been quilting bees or tea parties became storytelling sessions about our experiences as marginalized humans. Some of our conversations were like re-runs of "Queen for a Day," that most bizarre of 1950s television programs, in which women nearly destroyed by ill luck, family disease and repeated tragedy competed to tell the worst story of misery, and the audience applauded for the most affecting tale, and amid sobs and cheers presented the pitiable woman with a crown, two dozen long-stemmed red roses, and a new washing machine with a year's supply of detergent. So all of us graduate students shared stories, each worse than the last. In these contests I could never win the detergent.

I continue to read avidly about sexual difference, but my brain and gut have never acknowledged the essentialist stance. The differences are too subtle, and the exceptions are by the millions. To the church fathers who judged my menstrual cycle as constituting my lesser status, I contend: I did not spend one-fourth of my life incapacitated by an uncontrollable flow, and soon, very soon, the bleeding will end altogether. Am I no longer woman? To the feminists who rank women as more nurturing than men, I ask: are the countless people in which such personality predispositions are reversed essentially distorted human beings? To all maximizing tendencies, whether in Aristotle or Mary Daly, I shake my head. If men and women are to a maximum degree different—as popular literature would have it, from different planets—why should church and society value them equally and treat them the same? Do people imagine that this time around "separate but equal" will work? How will the law determine just how much female or male a particular human is? That a woman's hormones may lessen her directional abilities or that high levels of testosterone may increase a man's aggression is hardly warrant for women to be ditsy or men to be savage. Human society is often about the task of taming individual nature for the good of the community. I call myself a minimizer. Without denying the reality of sexual difference, obscure or ill-defined though it may be, I minimize it. I and Lucretia Mott.

Usually we use the term proto-feminist to describe women of the past who despite their androcentric assumptions accomplished feminist goals. But Lucretia Mott, nineteenth-century Philadelphia Quaker, was genuinely a feminist, arguing eloquently and campaigning relentlessly for the equality of women and men. At that time in America, both church and society devoutly proclaimed separate spheres; women were touted as closer to God than men, for women were closer to children, who were closest to God of all. Factories required labor more degrading than had the farm or the cottage industry, and many people argued that at least women should not stoop to such dehumanizing tasks. Women with stereotypically "feminine" personalities—a nurturing manner, a patient disposition, a submissive spirit—were lauded as the salvation of men, who were licensed to become more aggressive in the factory and more distant from the hearth. Mott rejected this entire worldview, lecturing against its seductiveness.

Mott's Christian faith supported her minimizing tendencies. Like other Quaker women, such as Margaret Fell, Sarah Grimke, and Angelina Grimke, she argued from Genesis 1 that men and women are created equally in the divine image and from the New Testament that Jesus' ethical teachings were directed equally toward women and men. "You are the light of the world," says the Sermon on the Mount, and Mott argued that Jesus didn't say, "You males." Without a male clergy or the inherited rituals of male dominance—Quaker wives did not vow obedience to their husbands, Quaker daughters were educated as many years as were sons—Quaker women could approach a parity between the sexes a century ahead of the dominant culture. Mott was insistent that women were independent moral agents: women were to get off their charming pedestal so they could join the men in trudging through the streets campaigning for peace and justice.

Recently I have discovered another minimizer in the philosopher Hélène Cixous. In contrast to some French feminists who maximize sexual difference, equating gender with sex and judging this the primary opposition reigning over all, Cixous challenges such binary distinctions, which she claims "never make any sense." Meanings flow: "the one is not without the other."[4] And although Western literature and mythology and philosophy have focused on protecting the "I"—Cixous' French calls this "masculine writing" although she refuses to identify it with male authorship—she sees "feminine writing" as that which opens to the other. To the feminists who claim that androcentric language renders them speechless, Cixous suggests that language, far from being solely a patriarchal power play, is first of all the connection of the "m/other" with her infant, the opening to the other after the bodies of two have separated.

As a writer of American English, a language that no longer uses the categories of grammatical gender, I have a linguistic obligation to distance myself even farther than can French-speaking Cixous from the labels "feminine" and "masculine." To those who speak American English, the categories of gender are burdens from the beasts of the past. I say that both females and males can protect the I, both can open to the other. Perhaps more women are better at opening to the other: surely, such opening to the other is our overwhelming social need. But my feminism does not close me into a room with only other women. The other must be with me, or I am not fully me, and the other includes both other women and other men.

I have come to learn a good deal about how miserable have been and currently are the lives of many women. But I find it patronizing, to use an androcentric term, to suggest that my life of privilege corresponds to that of the starving refugee walking miles for water or the adolescent recovering from a clitoridectomy or the wife beaten up in bed simply because we have ovaries. I will not trivialize the incessant suffering of these women by likening it to my job search.

Yet Cixous' question is mine: "who are I?" I answer that to know my whole I, I must connect with the other, the other whose life is inexplicably different from mine, the other who is stepping on me, the other who is being run over by a bulldozer. And this answer arises not because of my anatomy but rather from my religious convictions. That is, I attend especially to those who suffer because as a Christian I am called to do so. I believe that God is with those who suffer, and if I want to get near to God, I'd better stand with those who suffer. Along with Lucretia Mott, I find in my religion no sanctification of natural difference, but rather the challenge to see as equally valued all God's people, without reference to social usefulness or brain capacity or body type. I have achieved much by self-development of the I. Let me now be more open to the other. I am I-who-I-are; for although we do not survive well without boundaries to the self, neither can we thrive deeply without embracing the other.

repelled by the horrors of religion

To begin the gentle celebration of my fiftieth birthday, I went with my husband for a short visit to Mexico, to explore dead religion, to observe living religion, to wonder at religion immoderate, even outrageous, even horrifying.

Farthest back in history were the unknown pyramid-builders of a thriving city named Teotihuacan. The builders, imitating the magnificent mountains that border the valley, constructed their pyramid of the sun the third largest in the world. Even the Aztecs assumed these temples had been built by the gods. All the depictions of shamans painted on the walls are of males. But for the sanctified carnage—the buried bones are aligned with the sun's movements—one-third of the sacrificed victims were female.

Next in history came the Aztecs, whose religious artifacts fill the anthropology museums. Upscale shops and poor vendors sell elaborate and cheap sun depictions for tourists to purchase. But I know that the Aztecs believed that the sun required human blood for sustenance, finding especially yummy human hearts beating fresh from their living victims, and so, even remembering our solstice dinners, I do not buy a sun.

The sixteenth-century Augustinian monastery we visited had an outside amphitheater in which the natives attended mass. Augustinian monks did not, as did some conquistadors, cut off the feet of the natives who refused baptism, but this fortress-like structure is hardly inviting. The church's interior is decorated with portraits of austere, off-putting Augustinian worthies, and in a side aisle in a glass coffin is the wax model of the dead Jesus still used during Holy Week. Yet families with infants in white frills are milling around in festive mood: it is clear that some baptisms are scheduled.

Then there is the basilica of Our Lady of Guadalupe.

Women's studies books trace a lineage that sounds highly likely, from the Aztec goddess Cihuacoatl, Mother Serpent, to the sixteenth-century image of Mary. However, the latest meticulously footnoted historical study indicates that, sad to say, Mary was not in fact seen by a goddess-worshipping Indian peasant in

1531. Rather, she was concocted in 1648 by Mexico's Spanish clergy and back-dated to the conquest. You see, the clergy had a pressing need to prove that the Mexican-born Spanish community enjoyed as high a social and religious status as that of the more recent Spanish immigrants. How better to achieve this upgrade, than for Mary to appear in Guadalupe, Mexico, just as she had done before in Guadalupe, Spain? Thus, once again, the male hierarchy found veneration of a goddess handy for their own self-aggrandizement, and the oppressed peoples of the land, all the Juan Diegos, were manipulated to support the desires of the upper class. Now when I see contemporary women appealing to Mary, I wonder if they know to what degree she has been invented by misogynist males. To sum this all up: the apparition of our Lady of Guadalupe was neither Mary nor a trans-mogrified Aztec goddess, since she never appeared at all.

My mind knows this disturbing history, this pathway laid down with centuries of human hearts. Yet my eyes watch Indian families "creeping to Guadalupe," inching on their knees at least the last mile of their pilgrimage to give homage to Our Lady. Many carry bouquets of flowers to lay before the image, which they believe either Mary herself or God painted. I think of Dostoevski's Grand Inquisitor commenting on our desire for miracles. The historical study of Guadalupe documents that in the sixteenth century a painting of Mary was acclaimed for being able to produce miracles. A century later, the people claimed that the painting itself had been miraculously produced.

I could see easily over the crowds of standing pilgrims, for nearly all were native peoples, a head shorter than I. Beneath the painting, the deacon was reading the gospel for the first Sunday after Christmas, the story from Luke about Mary's postpartum purification ritual—forty days after a boy child, eighty after a girl—with old Simeon and ancient Anna apparently camping out in the temple until they'd see God's arrival. I have sometimes likened myself to Anna, waiting for God to arrive, hoping this baby is it. Pyramid temples, the Jerusalem temple, Aztec altars, Augustinian churches, Spanish baroque altarpieces (they are outside my vocabulary to describe, although the guidebook called St. Prisca's "the finest church in Mexico"), Mary with her offering of two doves, the Indian woman with her flowers, me hearing the gospel of the Presentation, temples, temples, temples.

Sitting on our patio at a hotel made from a ranch built by Cortes himself—one of our kids said, "Oh, you're staying in Genocide Suite?"—I think about religion. Why did whoever first cook up the idea that the sun ate hearts? Why is that squat Mexican woman, lowering herself even more, creeping on her knees across the plaza towards an unreasonably revered painting? Why have some of us such a voracious hunger for symbolic meanings? Yet for many, religion has shrunk. No one excavating Philadelphia, despite its richness of religious heritage, will stand stunned at unbridled religion, as we do at Teotihuacan, where perhaps 200,000 residents aligned themselves with a bloated religion that ate people dead and alive.

I think of two nineteenth-century American feminists. Elizabeth Cady Stanton, Presbyterian turned deist, would say that I am no different from the creeping penitent, except that I am self-deceived as well. Organized religion, Stanton said, is always harmful, especially to women. Religion told women *ad nauseam* that our blood makes us dirty; religion was always sacrificing us one way or another to the male hierarchy or the deity, even when a goddess was commandeered into inspiring the sacrifice. But Sarah Grimké, devout Quaker, argued otherwise. For her, the self-flagellation was not God's fault or intent; indeed, God empowered women from within; and the religious community supported women as we stood upright, unyielding as a temple, dedicated to enacting justice for others.

I am a daughter of Sarah Grimké. Raised to be religious, I continue to be, since on the whole the practice has been life-giving. I believe that if God exists, God gives life without extracting our hearts as payment. I have had fun hanging around churches. The people there have all the same miseries and failings as the folks at the mall, but we share a common language and ritual which give at least some meaning to the temples, the malls, the misery, the failings. And within some of the religious people standing alongside me beat profoundly loving hearts.

But from my vantage point, I see lots of women whose experience is other, for whom religion is like a safe deposit box, all locks and little air. Although I do not know to what degree the Mexican woman on her knees is enlivened by the Guadalupe ritual, I think of all the women who believe the bullshit they are taught, imagining that God shovels it their way, the women who wait patiently in line to have their hearts removed. When I was in fourth grade, I asked my Lutheran school teacher whether my Catholic friend Rosemary would get to heaven. He said no, she wouldn't, because she prayed to Mary. Though only ten years old, I thought to myself, well, he's wrong. Why did I know, even as a kid, that he was wrong, and that I could shake the dust of malignant religion off my feet? Surely if Christianity is to survive among contemporary women capable of designing their own destiny, it must evoke the spirit of Sarah Grimké. It must trust that God is not the author of misogyny, thriving on the carcasses of one woman after another.

(But. There is always a But. Can we finally exonerate God? Is God helpless to stop the slaughter? Yes. No. But.)

Perhaps being raised a Lutheran has helped me avoid the executions. Martin Luther, obsessed with religion, smitten by God, was a colossal religion-basher, hypercritical of the religious ideas and practices of his culture, chastising the church's leaders in uncontrolled, even scatological, rhetoric. The trick, of course, is both to bash and to revere, and to know when to do which.

drawn by the symbols of religion

As a child, I occupied myself during long sermons pouring over the seldom-used pages of our *Lutheran Hymnal*, which included the lists of biblical readings and prayers for saints' days. In that very Protestant, very male book, only one woman was honored with a day of her own: Mary Magdalene. So I'm glad to learn as an adult that in all likelihood this woman actually existed: not all "saints" are so lucky. We know her, not as would be customary for the first century by who her husband was, or her father or son, but only by herself: her Hebrew name Miriam, she lived in Magdala, a town on the shore of the Sea of Galilee.

Paul does not mention her, but Mark and Matthew place her at the cross and resurrection. Luke, who typically takes away with one hand everything he gives to women with the other, wrote that before she became a follower of Jesus, she had had seven devils. John's tradition, however, reveres her as the first witness to the resurrection. Some decades after the gospels were written, a concerned scribe added a happy ending to the book of Mark and used the opportunity to reiterate that this famous Mary character had been, after all, only a possessed woman. This is all the biblical gospels say about Mary of Magdala.

But thanks to scholars studying every extant manuscript, we now know that some second-century gospels describe her as a leader in the church. Others grant her something even more prized: intimacy with Jesus. This Mary of the gnostic Christians now has her cheering section, women who, disgusted with texts that give disproportionate honor to men, laud Mary Magdalene as Jesus' intimate companion and reverence her memory as an alternate way to know the mysteries of God.

Next came the catechetical Mary. The sixth-century Pope Gregory wanted an alluring image of repentance from sin and renunciation of the body. So although the third-century Hippolytus had honored Magdalene with the title "the Apostle to the Apostles," Gregory in one of his fits of organization and simplification preached that Mary of Magdala was the sinner woman who wept at Jesus' feet. Thus he ended up lumping together the New Testament's already small set of believing women into only two who mattered: the virgin Mary and the whore Mary.

The faithful were to take their pick. In countless Christian churches, both Marys are depicted at the foot of the cross: the older one enveloped by a silent grief, just as her frame is wrapped in its dark blue cloak, the younger one hysterical, her loose red hair and off-the-shoulder dress a sign of her life's excesses. Here's your option, said such art to women: be a weeping womb, or a screaming open body—not a charming choice, especially for women whose options were minimal and whose bodies were forced, and my resentment is so huge it is like a stone closing up the doorway to the tomb.

I see such images, along with many others, as androcentric, even misogynist, and I reject them as religiously significant. I want the impossible: to whitewash all those sobbing whores on church walls throughout the world. That men should have chosen the female prostitute as an emblem of personal sin is cruel, granting what we know of prostitution—that it results from economic necessity, personal tragedy, male incontinence, androcentric morality, even in the nineteenth century the desire of middle-class households for some kind of birth control. Not personal sin, but human misery is what the prostitute embodies. But I know that those parish committees, who would not welcome actual prostitutes to their pews, will spend piles of money to refurbish the paintings of this provocative prostitute on their walls. I will not succeed in convincing them that they are slandering a noble witness to the resurrection.

But next came Magdalene the legend. We can now read about the con job perpetrated by the eleventh-century Abbot Geoffrey who wanted the tourist trade—oops, the repentant pilgrims—to direct their prayers and coins to Vezelay, France. The nonsensical tales of how Mary Magdalene lived in France and how her bones moved here and there, bones which by the way were never displayed to the sometimes skeptical penitents, are worthy of an Indiana Jones film. But the cult of sexy Mary of Magdala overcame fact, logic, and integrity. The Romanesque church in Vezelay, with its immense narthex large enough for all the penitents to crowd into, its orange-tinted stone, its capitals depicting monsters and saints, mythical heroes and biblical characters, the signs of the zodiac and trees of life, is like a radiant golden embrace welcoming us all. The building is aligned with the earth's movements around the sun, so that at the summer solstice the sun shines on the center of the main aisle. Of all the churches I have visited in sixteen countries, the church of Mary Magdalene in Vezelay is one of my two favorites.

There are more Magdalenes. Magdalene the contemplative, sitting near her alabaster jar in a fifteenth-century middle-class house reading her psalter, was a favorite Dominican image. Now, following the recurring pattern of cutting down centuries of out-of-control imagination in order to allow new growth to thrive, contemporary believers are nurturing an independent Mary—Magdalene the liberated woman. Relying on no man, she was open to visions that men found harder to glimpse, and she was free to join, perhaps to lead, an itinerant religious society. When I needed a biblical story to depict what preaching is, I chose Mary of Magdala running joyfully from the tomb and proclaiming the resurrection, her joyous astonishment indicating not the touch of a man but an encounter with God. ("Touch": too many recent hymns talk of the touch of God. Is God like a teacher afraid of a lawsuit, or a child summoning courage to stroke a dead bird? Sometimes God comes as lightning, sometimes an embrace, too often a void: but for me seldom as a touch.)

This is how religious symbols work. The gospel writers are describing the influence of Jesus, and so Mary is remembered as a follower. The gnostics seek secret knowledge, and so to Mary is revealed the most profound divine mysteries. The pope hopes to teach, so Mary becomes a catechetical tool. The abbot lusts for the relic trade, and so Mary ascends into legend. The Dominicans desire an image for themselves as students of the word, and we feminists want an image for ourselves as liberated women. We make of the image an expression of our ideas. When we encounter the variations on Magdalene, we are encountering the church, which always has and always will include both the wild woman and the self-aggrandizing cleric, both the faithful scribe and the girl at prayer. Some symbols are spacious enough to contain much, and Mary Magdalene is one such world of symbol.

I am drawn by and into this imaginal life of the religious symbol. I prefer a museum visit to a mountain hike, an engraved gold locket to the flower pressed inside. I carefully deliberated over which image of Magdala to hang up in my office. For I know that images, like magic mirrors, alter what they reflect. How can the chaste narrative of Mary Magdalene in John 20 supplant our memory of that brazen tattooed gypsy named Mary Magdalene in the movie *The Last Temptation of Christ*? Should I hang up a poster of Fra Angelico's luminous lover in the Easter garden? the redhead reading her breviary? or a photo of the wooden santo in the Albuquerque church, an unadorned woman holding in her outstretched hands the image of the Risen Christ? I know that while the people—usually those in power, the bishops, the tenured faculty—create the images, the images in turn create the people, both their creators and all the others who look.

I know I am fascinated not only by the religious symbols themselves but also by the human endeavor of symbol-making. My favorite definition of what distinguishes the human animal from others is our symbol-making ability. We humans place flowers in the grave of our dead; we wear adornments to display our identity; we meet to feast on the darkest day of the year. When I had cats, I mounted a Native American hand-carved wooden salmon two inches above their food bowls. But I know that, alas, the cats cared only whether there was food in their dishes. They did not evidence any interest in Ultimate Meals, Perfected Food, Salmon Heaven. They just ate.

But we humans construct what W. B. Yeats called "the artifice of eternity."[5] And despite my irritation, even disgust, with Pope Gregory, I still wave at him over the centuries, one builder of the artifice to another. My ability to formulate a feminist Christianity with all its requisite feminist symbols is the same ability mastered by old Abbot Geoffrey, whose creation of a preposterous Magdalene legend rivaled the construction of the breathtaking basilica itself. Perhaps it is my delight over this ability that tempers my rage at androcentric imagery, for even I have to give those guys credit for their conscious and unconscious ability to see patterns, to invent designs, to make comparisons, to create meaning, and so to help humans imagine a golden pathway beyond the gutters they walk along each day.

But there was a real woman back there, cooking her daily meals, washing out her monthly rags, walking through Galilee and Judea. Of her means of support, her sex life, her family bonds, her psychological state, we know nothing. But as a witness to the resurrection she deserves our respect. However, simultaneously, we'll shape her into our story, writing new paragraphs, burning some of the old pages. Yet whenever we torch traditional symbols—and sometimes we must—we are scorching living Christians, for the symbols disgusting to me are life-giving to others. Since the Gregorys and Geoffreys are not dead yet, I must light my fires with care.

especially the ubiquitous tree of life

I discovered the tree of life in 1975 in a New York art museum. There for the first time I saw Hannah Cohoon's spirit drawing of her vision of July 3, 1854, "a beautiful Tree, bearing ripe fruit . . . that grows in the Spirit Land."[6] Her religious vision has landed in the public domain by now, for it is frequently reproduced, a logo for antique shops, a design on stationery, the pattern on jewelry and tote bags. You've seen it: the short trunk and gossamer branches mystically bearing up huge checkered dark green leaves and enormous dotted deep green and orange flowers.

Although decorative art as we know it was forbidden in the Shaker utopian communes, in the 1840s and 1850s some dozens of the women had visions from Holy Mother Wisdom and were permitted to record them, making designs of the detailed images, metaphoric tags, and pious sayings. Most of the spirit drawings resemble the sampler dated 1819 that is hanging on my dining room wall: animals here and there, flowers between, words around, and a grand central tree. I'm not surprised that the Shaker visions took on the shape of the samplers the women had embroidered as girls: most of us perceive our inspirations from the beyond clothed in the attire of our time. Only with our own words can we speak of what we've encountered. But Hannah Cohoon's drawings—she drew also the Blazing Tree, every leaf edged in flame—are not charming samplers. Her works are art, Shaker prohibitions notwithstanding, and like a true Western artist, laying aside the Shaker naming practice of Sister This and Brother That, she signed her masterpieces with her full name.

Many spirit drawings, whether sampler-style or masterpiece, utilize the leaf or tree as the central image. For, like others of the communitarian experiments sprouting up all over the nineteenth-century American countryside, the Shakers were confident that their utopian communes were the beginning of the kingdom of God, the inauguration of the Promised Land. Giving their farms names like Holy Grove, Holy Land, Wisdom's Paradise and City of Love, the believers had moved beyond the cross of Christ, for they were already enjoying the heavenly tree of life.

Shaker idealism does not captivate me. Nathaniel Hawthorne was right in *The Scarlet Letter*: all too soon each enthusiastic experiment in communal living requires a graveyard and a prison. But the tree itself enthralled me, sending me hiking over the centuries, into many Christian cultures and throughout other religions, and I have seen trees everywhere. I treasure Pennsylvania's autumn colors. I have stood under California's redwoods. I read about the cedar, the tree of life for Canada's northwest coast native people, and over our mantle is an Aboriginal painting of the pandanus palm, the tree of life in Australia's northern territories. In Sweden, among all those Bronze Age rock carvings of phallic warriors spearing animals, we found a prehistoric evergreen tree engraved next to a monstrous beast. When in Britain a millennium ago Saxon masons constructed stone churches for the Normans, they carved a tree over the doorway of one church after another. In Rome, at the garden cloister of St. Paul's Outside the Walls, each stone column is carved to represent a unique tree. Our collection includes tree rugs and mugs, tree prints and plates, tree sweaters and aprons, tree pendants and earrings. One friend calls our home the grove. And when at a hotel thousands of miles from Philadelphia I entered our room and saw a print of a man climbing down a tree to greet a woman sitting underneath, I knew I was at home.

But natural trees—even the moss-adorned temperate rainforests that pulsate with vibrant greens and grow in your mind forever after—are, like me, only alive for awhile. Ya live for awhile, and then ya die. Thus many trees of life reach toward the supernatural: a Currier and Ives heavenly tree with each fruit labeled as one of the virtues; a Mexican tree candelabra with naked Eve and Adam still happily surrounded with leaves and flowers; a yarn painting depicting the Huichol's vision-granting peyote plant. I think of the Buddha's Bodhi tree of enlightenment—a fig tree, the same as Augustine's; the four-plant stalk, with corn, maize, squash and tobacco all in one, on the Navaho sand painting; the burning bush that Marc Chagall created for Christian church windows. Indeed, although the cross with a bleeding Christ was all I had been taught, the church as a whole knew better, and though the stranger saw a dead man on a pole, the believer saw a magnificent, mysterious tree with twelve fruits, different each month, with all the birds of the air finding nest on the crossbeam. Do visit the church in Lohja, Finland, where the fifteenth-century biblical paintings that cover every inch of the church's interior walls and ceiling are placed between swirling branches, leaves and flowers up each pillar and around each arch, interconnecting all the images, with us in the pews, into the Jesse tree surrounding the main portal.

Poets remind us that the deepest images—the sea, the mountain, the monsoon, a woman's womb—signify both life and death. Living, even for a woman,
is not one flower after another. Indeed, while many women tout their monthly
flow as the red fruit of the tree of life, my menstrual malfunctions would have
killed me several times over, had not modern medicine held back death. So I read
with grim understanding that the guidebooks, sold in eastern cities to advise the
nineteenth-century pioneers for their westward trek, urged the women to get
pregnant before they set out; bouts of nausea, even the danger of miscarriage,
were nothing compared with the plight of a monthly flow. For only blood contained is life: blood flowing, whether from a dying man or a healthy woman, is the
end of life. I deem it an illusion that women are somehow more desirous or capable of life than men. Women as well as men have both life and death running
through their veins.

And so I need both, the tree and the cross: and only as both can either one be
hearty enough to stand. The cross by itself can become an icon to death, an acceptance of helplessness before the abyss, a picture of only the Buddhist first Noble
Truth that life is suffering, with no Eightfold Path as solution. However, the tree
by itself can be a Romantic dream, the fantasy that Mother Nature protects us
and gives us happiness, the sign of the short-lived Shaker chimera. The tree can
be the place to hide when we are being called into the house to do our chores.

There's a story in Numbers 17 that is, on one level, yet another tedious chronicle of patriarchy. The narrative tells the story of which man from which tribe is to
be chosen as religious leader in Israel. But the story is also a tree-of-life tale:
overnight, Aaron's staff—was it a shepherd's crook? a walking stick? a cudgel? a
magic wand? a scepter?—sprouted both pink and white blossoms and ripe almonds.
Flowers and fruits grow out from the long dead wood. I'll disregard the patriarchal
narrative and grab onto the flowering image itself, hoping that the newly alive
branch will be sturdy enough to support me as I walk. The tree of life is here, I say.
But finding it somewhere in the church's concrete and cardboard clutter is quite an
undertaking. "Undertaking"—an odd word, usually associated with boxing up and
burying dead bodies, I use to suggest the opposite: exhuming what has been erro-
neously buried alive, planting and watering what can blossom and bear.

with the serpent goddess out on a limb

According to some interpretations, the two trees in the garden of Eden are one. Both the tree of life and the tree of knowledge of good and evil are the one tree in the midst of the garden. If so, then entwined in the branches of my tree of life is the serpent. She might not be easy to spot: her green coat shimmers with the rustling leaves, her movement easily mistaken for the motion of the wind.

The book of Numbers records a startling ancestral memory of the Israelite people. The official version of the story says that the people were nomads, living in the Sinai, but they hankered after the ease of urban life, even the slavery of the Egypt they had escaped. The narrator says they complained against God, and in punishment God sent "burning serpents" to poison them to death. In desperation they pleaded for divine mercy. Moses then fashioned a huge "burning serpent" out of bronze and put it up on a pole. Moses instructs the people: if they "look at" the serpent on the pole, they will live.

As a child I did not see the incongruities of the story: Moses had a smelter in his tent? I remember the illustration of this story in my Bible study textbook, the women languishing half dead at the foot of a high cross, looking for all the world like medieval Marys swooning at the feet of the crucified Christ. Indeed, that was the point. We were taught that this serpent story "prefigured Christ," occurring in Israelite history mainly so that over a millennium later the author of John's gospel could write, "Just as Moses lifted up the serpent in the wilderness, so must the Son-of-man be lifted up." But we can't think that way any more, as if Israelite women agonized from snake bite in order to resemble Mary Magdalene. Long gone are the days of naively imagining all of world history to be a Gothic arch under construction, rising block by block up to the keystone Christ, and then it is finished. The Christian mind cannot be this small any longer.

About the serpent we now know—how many biblical scholars knew for how long but avoided reflection?—that many ancient Near Eastern cultures worshipped the serpent goddess. Imaged as a primordial dragon, or a grand female holding serpents, or a snake in a tree, or a snake on a pole, she lives and dies and lives again, renewing the face of the earth. Brave clergy now admit in their sermons that this story in Numbers 21 is indeed a memory of Israelite goddess worship. The people were dying, and looking up in reverence to the everlasting serpent, they lived. Some scholars suggest that the serpent goddess on her pole had an honored place in the Israelite temple for centuries, and only eventually did the monotheistic purists uproot the pole from its planting in the holy place. Perhaps it was these same purists who rewrote one of their neighbors' creation stories, in which the serpent in the tree grants a woman wisdom: they reversed it, rendering the serpent evil, the tree evil, the woman evil, and her wisdom a knowledge of evil.

However, the serpent continues to attract. She made her way around the globe, and still today Australian Aborigines describe the Creator as the Rainbow Serpent who comes from the land and returns to the land, ensuring the earth's fecundity. Contemporary readers pour over art history volumes and anthropological studies and Jungian picture books, drinking in the serpent goddess as if she is the cup of life. Wouldn't a tantalizing creative serpent in a bountiful tree be a more wholesome image of divinity for women, perhaps also for men, than a man dying on a cross?

Well, there a number of different ways to proceed in answering this question.

First, about goddess worship: by revering the serpent in the tree, one might be asserting that a goddess is better than a god. Each semester I encounter a few students who make this claim, young women who, I discover, know nothing of the world's goddesses except docile smiling Mary. Kali, with her necklace of human skulls, they do not know. Cihuacoatl, demanding human sacrifice, they never met. The goddess imagined by these students is the kitchen goddess of the nineteenth century's separate spheres: men are in charge of filthy machines and family discipline, women are in charge of clean clothes and wholesome meals. A kitchen goddess is, well, nice. She loves life, she ensures health.

I have come to regard Nasty-God-Nice-Goddess as an adolescent girls' rendition of religion, the female version of a "No Girls Allowed" sign posted on a boys' club door. It belongs on the shelf with Cinderella, and I am bewildered when mature adult women adopt such a goddess myth. When I read it in student papers, I suspect a nascent infantilism underneath the nostalgia for the perfect mother, or perhaps the virgin attitude of a woman who has never known herself in creative ecstasy with a man. In contrast, in their polytheisms the ancients knew to place their gendered divinities on both sides of the chasms of drought and monsoon, childbirth and maternal death, virginity and mating. They knew that to grant healing from snake bite, the goddess had to be Snake Bite Itself. She had to have known death, indeed to have borne death, to be able to take it back into herself and survive.

Those women in first-world countries who have adopted goddess worship have a somewhat different understanding of gender than college students tend to have. They know the deity to be beyond niceness. Their claim is, rather, that to know their self, to realize their potential, to withstand male violence, women's image of the divine must be like themselves: female. Power, whether to create or to destroy, comes through gender lines. It is as if the god of their monotheism, preferring males, being wholly unlike females, cannot be imaged by them and cannot include them. Only a goddess can grant them autonomous life.

The assertion that women's self-esteem flows from goddess worship is a new twist to old religion. For millennia, goddesses have presided over unassailably patriarchal cultures. So although it is true that in many cultures a male deity authorized male dominance, a female deity in and by herself did not insure high status for women. Either way, god or goddess, most women ended up underneath the men. I have come to think that not the religion but the socio-economic patterns— where was the food supply, what was the division of labor, how much energy did child-rearing take—determined how women's contribution to society was valued. I am struck by the data that Shaker communes established patterns of sexual parity several decades before their prayers called God Mother: sometimes our life changes before our minds do.

But let us return to the contemporary dilemma of constructing a religion that empowers women. As a minimizer living in the electronic age, I do not advocate separate religions for the sexes, a god for the men and a goddess for the women, Father for the males and Sophia for the females, as if my self must be projected into the skies in order for me to stand up straight on the earth. I imagine the deity beyond gender, the divinity beckoning us beyond ourselves into the other. I join with others in a monumental task of the next several centuries—describing God with many metaphors, images with and without gender, all partial pictures, only glimpses of the divine backside, each expression not the divinity itself but only the air moving when God breathes. A goddess may grant a situation novel to us, but I think she cannot by herself birth the new world.

But back to the serpent in the tree. The point might be pantheism. By revering the serpent goddess, one might be suggesting that the life of nature is all the life there is. The fecundity of the soil, the natural cycles of the seasons, the shedding of the serpent's skin, my monthly flow, these are divine. Wholesome life requires that we embrace the life and the death of the tree, joyfully confident that my brain will someday recycle as a leaf. Some women express this pantheism by talking about the goddess of the self. If the life around and in us is all the life there is, then I am goddess.

Often I reason that the natural world is all there is. But I choose to believe and to live as if there is more, a dimension beyond the natural cycles that gives a second, a third, yet another, level to what I see. I choose a religion beyond the natural. I will not get gushy about nature, claiming it to be more than it is. Knowing what science has discovered about amoral Mother Nature—eat or get et—I will not divinize her. And I cannot trust in the goddess who is me. Her power, it seems to me, is in direct proportion to the health and affluence of the woman in whom she resides. The Kenyan doll on my knickknack shelf, made of banana leaves: she mashes cassava with her pole in her clay pot. I want in religion more than the life of the banana tree, more than the life of the vulnerable woman.

And the detractors? By cursing the serpent in the tree, one might be claiming that father-god is better than serpent-goddess. Christians have taught that the goddess is evil, or does not even exist, or that the serpent in the tree can signify only the cycle of life and death, while the father-god conveys mercy. So I was raised to believe. But I no longer unequivocally assert this. Yes, father-god encompasses some divine truth, and in many world religions, both men and women have honored this image. But father-god has also meant that children are afraid and women are punished and men assume divinity. Father-god cannot by itself solve the religious dilemma, cannot answer to every agony. Such a god ought not replace the life of the tree. Such a god must, like the Hindu women, hug the tree.

A final group of interpreters includes me. The serpent on the pole is Christ on the cross.

For the feminist Christian, the meaning of the crucified Christ cannot filter through masculine sexuality. If Christ is about God becoming male, the crucifixion will not include me at all: indeed, following upon their oppressive church experience, this is what many post-Christian feminists claim. Oh, the confusion wrought by the androcentric word "man"! For even the theologians we call the church fathers taught that Christ became not male, but human. "What was not assumed cannot be redeemed" was the phrase often repeated to indicate that God became, not male, not half human, but wholly human, so to save the whole human race. Christ on the cross is meant to be about us all, women and men, acknowledging the reality of death, about our identifying with all those who suffer, about our realizing that we, too, will someday be on a cross. I mean never to worship death or to glamorize martyrdom. I mean, like the ancient Israelites, to look death, both male and female, straight in the face. The burning serpents are always slithering around our toes. Focusing on the serpent on the pole is one way to say, yes, death is hereabouts, around me, up my legs, in myself.

The serpent on the pole is an alternate image of Christ, the Christian message seen from a different angle, another facet of Calvary. There are lots more images of Christ, some already traditional: the yearling lamb sacrificed in the temple, the warrior dead on the battlefield, the noble volunteer substituting for the criminal. One task for feminist Christians is to offer far more inviting images of Christ, far more convincing interpretations of that long-ago execution. For we feminist Christians will not wallow in death, taking a corpse with us to bed. I heed the death only because of faith in what Christians call the resurrection. The erect cross has its meaning only because of the womb of the empty grave.

Thus for me the goddess is not renounced. She is recognized, even ratified, as one divine image of both death and life, the poison and its antidote, snake bite and salvation. The story in Numbers suggests that even the chroniclers of the Hebrew stories conceded the point: goddess and god, Asherah and Yahweh, are one. Hear, O Israel: God, our Living God, is one.

If some goddess worshippers dismiss my interpretation, most Christian systematic theologians will dismiss me altogether. They will warn me of heresy, I will be censured for incorporating pagan imagery. But to my conservative baptized colleagues I say: If the crossbeam and the arms of Jesus can't hold a serpent, they can't contain me. Don't be so distressed: the cross is big enough. The serpent and her tree are also there. Just look carefully; stand next to me: can't you see her in the light shining through the window from this side of the room?

reading a Bible written by men

B
eing Lutheran, my parish does not employ its own wisdom and preference to choose the biblical passages that are read and preached each Sunday. Along with an increasing number of Christians all around the world, Lutherans use a lectionary which is an ecumenically-designed list of biblical selections. For each Sunday and festival of the year, this three-year cycle of readings appoints four selections, which usually include a reading from the Hebrew Bible, a part of a Hebrew psalm, a passage from one of the early Christian apostolic letters, and, as the climactic reading, a selection from one of the four gospels, Matthew, Mark, Luke, and John. The Hebrew Bible and its psalms were written, give or take, 2500 years ago, and the New Testament letters and gospels come from the three generations following Jesus' ministry. Except for a small number of pages which may have had a female author, the entire Bible was penned by men, and those men thought in androcentric terms, wrote in androcentric language and imagined androcentric metaphors.

Sunday after Sunday I hear stories about famous men, poems attributed to men, essays written by men, and a communal memory about Jesus as recorded by men. Few women are remembered for something other than birthing a famous man, attending to a famous man, or finagling their way through the patriarchal system. I recall my doctoral studies in literature in the 1970s, before diversity in curriculum challenged the reign of the dead white males. Each hundred pages of Flannery O'Connor was buried alive by two thousand pages of William Faulkner. Walt Whitman, not Emily Dickinson, merited an entire course. Finally, my doctoral exams over, I, who adored the convoluted prose of Henry James, read the journal of Alice James, his unbalanced sister. Here the convolution was not in studied sentences but in her troubled self. Beside every great man is a woman driven mad? It was a long time before I picked up another novel written by a man. Weekly now I read the book reviews, and of the unceasing production of novels written by men I find myself thinking, I've read that book before.

Back to the Sunday readings. I am not shocked by the maleness of the biblical readings. Indeed, I served on one of the committees that labored to make the selections. Our committee could not insure, as I do in constructing a syllabus, that half the readings were written by women. We could not balance passages describing God as king with others in which God is queen. The biblical writers did not share our current sensibilities, and their corpus cannot meet such requirements. Thus I sit there and listen, and wonder: how can this corpus of largely androcentric writings have meaning for a contemporary woman? In universities, the English faculty fight it out: Shall the department continue to give Milton a course of his own? Ought we analyze *Paradise Lost* with feminist hermeneutics? Or should we ditch the poem for women's diaries? The crisis is sharper in the church than in the academy, since most Christians believe that the androcentric Bible is, if not our only, at least our primary text.

The first question to ask is how one hears the Bible, sexist passages or not. I was raised a fundamentalist. The picture in my fourth grade Bible history text showed God beaming down from heaven the very words into the pens held by holy men. The gospels referred to God as Father; the writers had received their words from God; and so we too must call God Father. For a fundamentalist, biblical language is God's truth, and thus it is mandated for church use. Only the "truth" that God is Father will set us free.

I have, however, a luminous high-school memory of taking an evening Bible course designed for Sunday School teachers—not, I realize, what constitutes a treasured adolescent memory for most people. A dynamic campus pastor introduced us to the historical-critical method of biblical studies. For the next twenty years, I would have said that although the biblical writers were not taking dictation from God, their words, like most mothers, were "good enough." Their language had become canonical for believers. The gospel writers called God Father, and as a church member, I accepted that language as my own.

When I was thirty-five, I spent a summer plowing through Paul Ricoeur's theory of metaphor. Thanks to Ricoeur, I now think of the author of the gospel as recording the metaphors of a believing community. Whoever he or she was, "John" preserved the voice of a specific community, one passionate to convey to others its experience of God's grace, a grace that is always beyond words. The vocabulary of that ancient community guides my speech, gives me sacred words, but does not limit my language. The Johannine community called God Father; I inherit that metaphor; I study its meaning in both ancient and contemporary communities; I know that one metaphor will not contain all there is to God; and I call God father, three-in-one, mother, rock, tree, mystery. The writer, although probably male, was not like a contemporary novelist flashing us his male imagination. Rather, the writer, a talented reporter, was assembling the community's scrapbook, handing down to future generations the metaphors sacred to a community, a community which came together after some women had a vision of their leader risen from the dead. These sacred metaphors can move mountains, can make the blind see, can open doors and let the imprisoned women go free. But the meaning of the metaphors is not always self-evident to the casual reader: think, for example, of the terms Messiah, Logos, Son-of-man. Much of this language is insiders' speech, which we must decode and translate.

I know that for the feminist who quits the church, the New Testament writers are dead white males, and those who adopt their language are choosing to be buried alive, their mouth stopped by stale air and growing mould. But I am still testing the metaphors. Some biblical metaphors I will pick up, hold in my hands, and see that the silverplate has worn off, the base metal is showing through. These I shut away in the drawer, or throw away altogether. But others, I discover, are sterling. And when we read the gospel of John in church, I realize that I am the woman at the well, I am the man born blind, I am the sheep needing protection in the fold, I am fruit growing on the vine.

I know that my considerable knowledge of the Bible is part of the life jacket that keeps me afloat on Sundays. I know, for example, that the most misogynist passages of the Bible, the Leviticus 18's and 1 Timothy 2's, are not ever read on Sunday mornings, for the church has long agreed with feminists that some of the Bible is unfit for public proclamation. But while I have managed to stay afloat on Sundays, I don't always enjoy the tempest. I see these mighty male metaphors come crashing toward me, and I have to take out my hymnal and crawl into a hymntext based on Hildegard of Bingen's writings to wait out the storm. When I weary of king-this-and-king-that, I recall all the narratives of the women giving birth, and I am revived.

I am upheld by the realization that religion is a communal vision. I am not, my prairie mother's notions notwithstanding, alone with my Bible facing a cyclone. The community was and is both male and female. My teachers were women and men, the authors I read women and men, the saints before me were both Perpetua and Martin Luther, I worship standing beside a man. I know that although in the first century it was men who recorded the stories, it was women who first witnessed the resurrection. In the fourth century, Libanius, the famed pagan teacher of rhetoric, instructor of the young John Chrysostom, ridiculed the Christian faith, for its doctrines were being taught, Libanius said, by "your mother, your wife, your housekeeper, your cook."[7]

However, the communal sense cannot confuse my critical faculties. I must still operate on the texts to excise their various cancers. That the Bible assumes a slave society does not mean that the contemporary Christian community can sanctify slavery. Nor, however, does our integrity demand that we jettison the historic text as a debased artifact from the past. The biblical passages that bless slavery are a poignant example of the massive, unending effort required for the hermeneutical task of interpreting the canonical texts in the world's religions. How does the living community read the ancient text? Is there life in Ezekiel's valley of dry bones? To the believing feminist the answer is yes: the bones will come together, bone to bone, and sinews will form, and skin will grow, and from the dead male bones will rise a new living people, women and men, a vast multitude.

Presently the church is littered with bones. The bones are all around the ground, the bones are inside ourselves, our very skeleton is part of the pile of bones. Indeed, I admit that our androcentric past is part of the strength of our backbones. But I want a female skeleton, with hips wide enough to cradle whatever I carry to term. So: we select what will live and toss what is dead, hoping we make the right choices. 1 Timothy 2, out; John 20, in. In some biblical texts, the marrow still flows. All is not dead.

symbols can smother

A t one point in my life I belonged to a Lutheran congregation that week by week was shrinking. Finally all that was left was a mutual admiration society of about eight like-minded people. I recall rushing out of the building at the close of one service in order to breathe deeply: the polluted air of the New York City streets was easier to take in than the smothering sense of shriveled symbols and narrow communal interpretation. As the assembly had shrunk, so had our access to vibrant symbols. I understand why some pseudo-Christian cults climax in suicide: there is, at the end, no air left.

Religious groups use symbols to express what is beyond expression. Symbols are concrete images, objects, and rituals that evoke abstract ideas or values, and when the symbols are many and diverse and multivalent, when many of us gather around the symbols to point out to each other their many facets, then the symbols can breathe out a radiance lively enough that we can all dance around in the room enjoying the air and light. But the symbols can be too few, or too flat, or too univocal, and when this happens in the church, naturally some folk will rush out of the room gasping for fresher air. Those who leave had better, however, attend carefully to their own future: replacing too constricted a Christianity with another limited worldview may be only switching from life under a rug to life under a carpet, novel at the outset, but finally suffocating in a not dissimilar way.

So here is the rug that women have been swept under: God is referred to as he. God is named Father and called King. We are saved by the man Jesus. Jesus chose men as apostles. Males are the thinkers and the leaders in the church. Men are essentially more human than are women, yet men can image the divine as women cannot. Eve was our evil mother, Mary an impossible goal. Women are created for sexual activity, which is unavoidably sinful. Women are to emulate Jesus by serving others. The church licenses social strictures on women, who are to obey male authority.

It is no wonder that many women throw off this chador and emigrate to a country that doesn't veil women. The wonder is, rather, that some women are not suffocating: some because they have expert survival skills, others because the symbols of their faith are not so stereotypically oppressive. Some of us are clever about cutting holes here and there, to get more air, to see the sights. I understand why some women leave the church, but I have expended most of my creative adult energies writing books and producing materials and addressing conferences and leading retreats urging exactly this: that the symbols need not be so small, they are not so small, here, look at this, look at it this way, there is room for us here, please stay with me here, we need only alter the light and shift the shadows, oh no you're looking at the trash pile, see here, here, is the treasure chest with gems for us all, an opal for you, a pearl of great price.

Just as knowledge of the Bible helps me survive sermons, so knowledge of church history gives me a ballroom in which to dance. I recall the Peanuts cartoon in which Lucy is to write an essay on church history; her first sentence is, "My pastor was born in 1947." Stifling, stifling. One way to read the church's history is to trace its symbolic switches. When the Christian church was small and struggling, God was the apocalyptic conqueror. When Christians dominated Western civilization, God was the exacting judge watching our every move. When this single cultural vision became blurred, the Reformation proclaimed God to be a loving father forgiving our every move. With the gradual disintegration of patriarchy, God the father is now fading, and believers are quarreling over which image can take its place. But if you know church history, you know that in the past God sang different songs than the slight ditty the choir is singing right now. If one's God is not too small and weak, then the infinite God can fill new spaces.

One complication is that what strangles one woman is exhilarating to another. The bridal veil: Is it a disgusting remnant of the days when a father wrapped up his daughter to sell sight unseen to another man for his son's use? Or is it a charming white pouf, a frame for the bride's smiling face, an aesthetic balance for the long full skirt? Signs are univocal: you see a red light and without thought you stop the car. However, symbols can go one way or another, the water in a mikvah, the water swallowing the Titanic, the mountain as the glorious pillar for the sky, the mountain as excruciating death to the explorer. Archetypes have enough meanings toward either death or life to go around: you can take your pick.

I am one of the women who most Sundays can breathe. Of course, I am meticulously selective in the churches I attend, for I chose to protect myself from carbon monoxide poisoning. On the occasions that I feel myself getting asphyxiated, I find I can turn my head away. I will not suffer under such small silliness. Such tiny symbols of ultimate reality, I say to myself, do not contain or constrain me, and when the worship flattens or the sermon shrivels, I transform myself from worshipper to observer. A person fascinated by religion, I can become an outsider, watching and wondering at an ecstatic voodoo trance or a pompous pontifical mass, while breathing deeply that the ritual has not to do with me.

Perhaps it was my parents coaching me to reject false authority, to rise above it into the air of God. I have been assisted also by my life-long love of metaphor. As a child I memorized poetry, and in graduate school I studied with a Pulitzer-Prize-winning poet and read all the great novels written in American English. And so it is second nature for me to probe the symbols of the church's poets and theologians and mystics. What did the Christian writers mean by their words? By "mean" I am not referring to some double-columned dictionary. Rather I ask: what was the palace they lived within? I read Augustine talking of God as rest and Catherine calling God her mad lover: which God is there for me today?

But even for me, with my confidence that somewhere in the trash pile is a priceless pearl, some things have got to go. Take Ascension Day. What with psalms extolling kings and Luke's men gazing up into heaven and Jesus rising up to his throne in the sky, I'm glad Ascension is a Thursday. It's not the day of the resurrection, and I don't have to go to church. I realize and teach that although the words of Ascension Day are filled with male hierarchy, they don't mean them. God's garden is bigger. But sometimes you don't have the will to explore, or there is not a compelling reason to muster the creative exegesis. So I skip Ascension Day, and I suggest to others that they do the same.

It is complex, how symbols breathe both life and death, in different amounts, to different people, whose needs change week by week, year by year. But we must never forget the fact that some people are smothered by religious symbols. Religion is intended to offer life in the face of our perpetual deaths. Religion is not around to provide yet another occasion of death. And so those for whom the church is a hovel consider leaving. But I hope they realize two things as they go: that not every available mansion is a healthy place to live and that some of us find the church more palace than hut.

or manifest the mystery

eligion approaches mystery with metaphor.
By mystery I do not mean, as in a murder mystery, a puzzle, a maze we muddle through, bumping into walls, the author God having plotted out all the surprise dead-ends. By mystery neither do I mean a wonder, the astonishment we feel while watching nature specials on public television and witnessing the ingenious ways that various species eat and mate and rear their young. No, by mystery I mean something other than the suspense until we know the final outcome or the respect we offer that which we do not understand.

Religion's mystery is the realm beyond our thinking and knowing. Mystery surrounds these inquiries: whether there is an ultimate reality; if there is, how we can connect ourselves with it; not how humans developed, but why; not the biology of human sexuality, but its powers and purposes; not the location of heaven, but the goal of consciousness and its actions. The scholar of religion, Rudolph Otto, had to invent a word to articulate religious mystery: numinous, he said, was the quality of emanating divine power, of evidencing a value beyond. I mean, of course, not a second level, as if what matters is a spiritual world behind the physical, as if what is essential casts light over the transient within which we live. That is all Platonism, and I am rigorously anti-Platonic. By mystery I mean what cannot be typed into the zeros and ones of the binary code. I mean the expanse between the yes and the no, the depths that our human mind seems unable to map, although periodically people tumble into it and emerge better people for the fall. If religion is not about these mysteries, it might as well close up shop. If all we need are ethical systems and positive reinforcement, there are more straightforward ways to achieve such humanistic goals than the circles and swirls of religion.

(A young woman explained that according to her therapist, before she can conquer her anorexia, she must identify its precise source. I am so ashamed, I am so ashamed, she said, I must know why I started doing this, I am so ashamed. And I thought, well, that therapist will make lots of money: as if this person can be spelled out in yes's and no's, and the source of her disease fully diagrammed on a screen, and then the problem can be solved, then healing can begin. I wish that religion could help this woman to imagine the mystery behind the self, and that perhaps Christianity could promise her grace, and that so supported, she could begin to live with and within her unfathomable self.)

Religion approaches mystery with metaphor.

Metaphor states not what is, but what isn't, and in the saying makes it so. Metaphor says the third thing, the space between, the paradox, and if the saying is strong and accurate, we see the old thing a new way. Paul Ricoeur teaches that all uniquely human communication is creative metaphor. Our speech applies one thing to another. Our words accumulate significance, from a known past to the unknown present. All our best words decorate the Christmas tree. A living language grows by metaphors. After all, in George Orwell's *1984*, when repressive government attempts to control all human thought, creative writing and all the implements used in creative writing are outlawed. After we read T. S. Eliot's "Let us go then, you and I,/ When the evening is spread out against the sky/ Like a patient etherised upon a table,"[8] sunsets are forever altered for us, and we look at nightfall no longer with a thoughtless sentimentality but accompanied by the ambivalence of human existence.

Beginning in the mid-thirteenth century and lasting until the printed Bibles of the Reformation, European Christians relied on a remarkable catechetical device that scholars call the *Biblia Pauperum* to teach the faith. First hand-drawn as manuscripts and later printed as blockbooks, these picture books proliferated throughout Europe, in Latin, old French, and old German, and their images were displayed on liturgical artifacts and painted on the walls of churches and monasteries from Scandinavia to Italy, England to Austria. The genre was a masterpiece of metaphor. In the center of each of the forty pages was a picture of an event in the life of Jesus. Encircling this were arranged eight other pieces: two pictures of Old Testament stories, chosen as being in some way parallel to the Gospel story; four quotations from the prophets or the psalms in some way related to the main story; several paragraphs of homiletical explanation; and a single summary sentence tying the page together. Sometimes the pieces were laid out in medallions, as if the page were a quilt; sometimes the scenes were drawn inside Gothic arches, as if by looking at the page, one was in church praying.

Let me give an example of how this metaphor works.

Since the first century, the Christian church has proclaimed the virgin birth. Any thinking feminist must face the origin and progress of this doctrine.

Matthew and Luke, the authors who narrate these stories, knew nothing about women's ovaries but believed, as did Western science until the eighteenth century, that the active male inserted into the passive female all that was essentially human in conception. Thus what the gospel writers seem to mean by the virgin birth is, despite current popular imagination, not that God fertilized Mary's egg, but that Jesus came wholly from God. The mystery that the narratives manifest is of the nature of Christ, not of the anatomy of Mary, and meditation on Mary's hymen has only got the church into paroxysms of nonsense, most of which spelled bad news for women, whose pregnancies, over which they had little control, rendered them ripped and sullied in contrast to the virgin's "undefiled" state. So what's a feminist to do with all this?

The images on the second page of each *Biblia Pauperum* offer one suggestion. The central picture is the stable scene, with Mary (in one group of blockbooks she is reading her breviary), Joseph, and the baby Jesus, along with the ox and the ass, imported as always from Isaiah 1:3. The two Old Testament stories illustrating the meaning of this birth are not about women's bodies, but rather are Moses seeing God in the burning bush and Aaron witnessing his walking stick bursting into blossom. Both stories are metaphors for the mystery, ways to say that God appears in surprising ways and in unexpected places. God is born a baby: the fire of God can burn but not consume; the wooden staff can flower overnight. I must admit that the homilectical sentences that I read on this page express the medieval celibate's obsession with the virginal state. But the metaphors provided by the images are more profound than the text. There is space in these metaphors for dancing.

The metaphors of the burning bush and the flowering rod do not, cannot, explain the mystery: they merely manifest the mystery. One believer points to the mystery, showing it to another. In witnessing to the mystery, one believer says the tomb is empty, another says that there was a vision of angels, another says we touched his wounds. But what is experienced remains a mystery. I see this mystery manifest in the creeping pilgrims at Guadalupe, in the continuous faceting of Mary of Magdala, in the forest of trees of life throughout religion and all over my walls, in the serpent herself grinning at me through the branches, in the records of first century Christians. But the task is not only to examine, sometimes wonder at, the poets' powers of metaphor. My task is to help construct a Christianity that can resonate with, animate, and inspire the contemporary feminist.

The prolegomenon is over. Let the constructive task begin.

about ultimate reality . . .

the mystery of One-in-Three

R eligion is supposed to be about ultimate reality. Now, of course, it often isn't; or rather, if that meager idea or foolish ritual or limited activity is your notion of ultimate reality, count me out. In the historic world religions, the various descriptions of ultimate reality have been sharpened up and polished down by centuries of thought and practice, and the hope is that these conceptions are intellectually challenging, emotionally fulfilling and ethically inspiring. And I say, anything said in the church about God that is stupid or stunted or stultifying says more about the speaker's view of things than it says about God.

The three historic monotheistic religions—Judaism, Christianity, Islam—all claim that in the first place this ultimate reality, identified as "God," is mystery. God is finally unknowable, beyond human conception, outside linguistic categories. One would think this goes without saying: by definition, the reality that is ultimate cannot be grasped by human minds or conveyed by human language. This truth is evident in Judaism's classic prohibition against drawing pictures of God or pronouncing the divine name. But lots of Christians have drawn and lectured God to death. You'd think, listening to some sermons, that God is a set of doctrinally-approved theses. And I say, if God isn't in the first place about mystery, you can just forget the whole thing.

Before me, two quotations, one from the fourth century, Augustine: "*Hoc ergo non est Deus, si comprehendisti*"[9] (If you comprehend what you are saying, you are not speaking God); and one from now, Hélène Cixous: "And one can sum up God in his name that means everything that I do not know what it means."[10]

The Christian method of suggesting divine mystery has resulted in the doctrine of the Trinity, and ironically this vehicle for mystery has occasioned more fatal accidents, especially for contemporary women, than perhaps any other aspect of the religion. For many feminists, "Trinity" has totally failed. Yet for others, including me, this doctrinal proposal, if presented profoundly, could be Christianity's most thoroughly feminist conception.

Let me begin by trashing, not the Trinity, but superficial, even witless, depictions of the Trinity. You look into these chests of language and imagery and you find them nearly empty, with no splendid jewels inside, only old dustballs, and you go get your featherduster, and there's the end of that.

I saw the supreme unacceptability in a Mexican church. I had never before seen this image, although countless Christians have lived and died with this as their "one God": three identical Renaissance-looking middle-aged men with their feet resting on the globe, on which was shown the garden of Eden, with the tree, Adam and Eve. God looks like Albrecht Dürer become Siamese triplets. Please, I ask, get your six feet off my tree. I read that in 1745, Pope Benedict XIV, a learned scholar with a modern interest in science, condemned and banned this image. That it still hangs in churches demonstrates that patriarchal images can be more potent than patriarchal officials.

If both Pope Benedict and I give the three men an F, the image I grew up under deserves a D-. The church in which I sat once, sometimes twice, a week for seven years of my childhood boasted murals that had been painted by a congregation member. This did not bode well for our religious imagination. The "one God" was three large figures, each pictured from the waist up: one a benign bearded old man; one a long-haired middle-aged man, with an astonishingly bare chest (did I see this as suggestive of sex, or only of summer trips to the beach?); and a figure cloaked in ermine, the face hidden in whiteness, with a radiant upraised hand. Lest I forget this wonderment, I have a picture of it still today, photographed on a Christmas card. And what grade shall we give to the painting on the chancel wall in the Lutheran church in Augsburg, Germany: God wearing the three-tiered papal crown? I am staggered that after nearly five hundred years of Protestantism, this depiction remains in place.

Yet not every woman reacts as I do. One American feminist Christian responded with great devotion to the classic depiction called "the Throne of Grace:" an old gracious man holding a crucifix, and at the top of the cross, mid-picture, rests a dove. This image does nothing for me. I look at it as at Shiva, someone else's image of mercy. Note well: not all feminists are alike.

In my tradition images are presented more often in hymns than on walls. Each Lent we got to sing late Reformation hymns of numerous stanzas in which the Father and the Son are chatting up in heaven about the mechanics of the substitutionary theory of atonement. In a final stanza the Spirit shows up to witness the conversation. Perhaps a thousand years ago, when it was thought that fathers owned their sons, the idea of a father giving up his son suggested magnanimous generosity. It now suggests parental child abuse. I think these hymns should now be locked up in ecclesiastical jails along with all other religiously dangerous artifacts.

My judgment is that the culprit in the doctrine of the Trinity is not the mystery of One-in-Three, Three-in-One, but the title Father. Belief in the Trinity is intended to praise the three as equal in the one, but the word father, hauled in from other religious systems and blessed by the New Testament, was too heavy a term. It swamps the ship of Three-in-One, replacing it with a raft with one male captain in charge. Many in the church have tried valiantly to proclaim the uniquely Christian ideas in the father language, stressing the doctrinal point that God is father of Jesus. And there is no question that for many people, the word father has indeed conveyed the idea that God is for us, rather than against us.

But lots else, not particularly Christian at all, has come along with the word. There's the biological error that fathers are responsible for procreation; the cultural pattern that fathers owned their children; the philosophers' use of the metaphor father to designate the Unoriginate Origin; Greco-Roman religion that called Zeus-Jupiter father. Even in the Hebrew Scriptures, God is father to King David in a way little different from how the deity is father or mother of various ancient Near Eastern potentates. It is ironic that the Christian God became popularly Father only in time to witness the weaknesses, and the weakening, of patriarchy. For, although in the Middle Ages God was primarily king and judge, it was after the Reformation that the title "father" grew in use, even as fathers were losing authority, until Protestant free prayers, all beginning "Father God," were prayed by nineteenth-century women choosing their own husbands and arguing for the vote.

I need say no more about this. Out there are dozens of books describing the insufficiency of a father God and advocating the burial of the title along with the patriarchy it represents. I do not, however, advocate that the title be entirely discarded. It needs considerable repair. It cannot be and do all its supporters claim. Yet it brings its historic significance to our assembly, and that is not nothing. Our tree has roots. The Christian faith is two millennia old and so is some of its speech. But there is no question that mainline Christians are using father language less and less, recognizing its limitations, alternating it with other terms. Yet all too often, in replacing father, the Trinity gets pitched, and this seems to me a mistake.

Trinity language is supposed to be about mystery. The faith proclaims that the one God is not a self-sufficient monad. Even God, the One, needs the Other in the self. Judaism has taught us that God is the "I Am": Christians, in meeting Christ and experiencing the Spirit, can call God the "I-who-I-are." This is not to say (I hear you, Descartes) that there is not the I, or the one God, but that the I, and the one God, must be plural in order to be a singular self. And there is more: in the Christian Trinity, the I-who-I-are has differentiation without subordination. Contrary to what gets suggested by the title father—that the father is prior to or greater than the son—the Three are coextensive, "equal in glory, coequal in majesty," the fifth-century Athanasian creed asserts. Many people have attempted a coequal dyadic relationship: but a coequal trio? Good luck. Only ultimate reality can long succeed in that.

The trick is to keep the three in balance.

Overstressing what's been termed "the First Person" might leave you with deism, one big god up in the sky, perhaps a sweet or dull creator who hasn't done much since, perhaps a judge who records your every good and evil deed in the great book in the skies. Overstressing the First can leave the deity up there and me down here and little connection between. Some people are glad for the gap, others ache for union.

Overstressing the Second presents me with Joseph Campbell's hero myth. The Jesus story by itself is only yet another male savior story: the man endures great perils in search of his goal, and though he dies, he comes to life again, flowers bloom in the spring, and I can too. He journeys from the little town Bethlehem to the city of Zion, from the stable to heaven, and so can you, especially if you are a man or a lucky woman. Yawn. For this myth, I do not need to go to church: I can watch Star Wars.

Overstressing the Third can result in pantheism. The spirit of life is in everything, in me, in the circle of my community, in the tree around which we dance. There is nothing beyond us to draw us into a holiness greater than ourselves. What you see is the sacredness there is. I am goddess.

But in brilliant balance nothing would be said of any one of the Three which does not include the truths of the other two. Each proposal corrects the others, moving it away from simplicity toward mystery. We call the First Cause God; in Jesus we meet God; through the life of our community we experience God. God is beyond, and with, and in. Now, that's a mystery.

The One-in-Three might signify something like this: The One is about transcendence, about being beyond the universe, the mystery that precedes the big bang and that remains after my death. I am, alas, thank goodness, not god/goddess; the ultimate reality is other than me, prior to me, and I must be in relation to it. From this One came all humanity, including the odd man Jesus. This Two is about incarnation: that deity doesn't stay resting off somewhere in heaven (whatever "heaven" means), located apart from the human sphere, but rather became human. Transcendence transforms human life. The Three is about communion, the bonded circle that animates, the shared life without which existence is meaningless. The Three affirms that the future of the One and Two is in us all. Now, that's a mystery.

This divine mystery leaves no room for the male chauvinist in church or society to style himself a chip off the old block God by being distant or domineering. Imitating God must be about including the other. God is not only the universal world tree: God is also a hanging tree, for as all humans, so even God dies: and God is also the fruit that the other picks off the tree, the lifejuice of the fruit that we share at table together.

Because of the Third, the deity is part of the I-who-I-are. Because of the Second, I see in Jesus the I Am. Because of the First, I am not the ultimate I. We strive to say it better. Paradox is not about sloppy thought, but about mystery. I know that Judaism has other ways to articulate this complex unity: I think of Martin Buber writing about I encountering God in the You. But "Trinity" is the way Christians do it.

Oh, there's decades, centuries, of reconstructive surgery the churches must undergo before our language about God is reshaped. But I'm in for the long haul. For there's hope, feminist hope, that this wracked up body still has some life in it. There's still milk in those breasts.

our Clothing

In a patriarchal world, it's easy to describe God. God is the peak of the triangle, the king ruling from the summit of the mountain. All things are assigned their spot in the pyramid: at the base are the stones then trees then animals then women then slave men then free men then ruling men then God; and if everyone holds perfectly still, crouching there on hands and knees, the structure will be stable, rising solidly into the air, nothing will topple, people don't fret about where they belong, and the deity reigns without contest from the throne on top. Although it's not much of a Trinity, this image of God showed up plenty in the Christian history, and is still invoked today.

According to patriarchy, knowledge of God trickles down from God at the top. Women have access to God only through the men, their fathers, husbands, rulers, priests, take your pick. A connection exists between women and God, but there's an exceedingly lengthy distance between them, and not a direct route, for along the way are required stops, the king and the priest and the husband. I recall my parents making a long distance phone call in the early 1950s to my grandparents in their tiny Minnesota town. You had to place the call with an operator, who then relayed the call to a second operator. Some time later our phone rang: the operators had finally put the connection through, and we shouted at my grandmother over the line.

But cracks developed in the monumental religious pyramid. My favorite is the mystic crack. After the year 1000, there arose more and more women who got off their hands and knees, thus causing minor or major upheavals in their corner of the pyramid. And what made them stand up tall were their mystical visions. The mystic has a revelation of God within: although these women maintained that their visions were wholly congruent with orthodox Christian belief, their revelations came not via the males or the things of males but directly from God. Some of these women authorized themselves to write, while the visions of others were recorded by their adherents. This short-circuiting of the Great Chain of Being, this unexpected manifestation of authority, recorded in the women's striking poetry and prose, was a significant preliminary step to both the women's movement in the West and the Reformation movement in the church.

One of these visions occurred on May 8, 1373, in Norwich, England. A woman we know as Julian—although that is not a woman's baptismal name, only the male saint's name given to the small church in Norwich where she resided as a solitary—gave up her name, and whatever else she had, or had lost, and lived in a room affixed to the outside of a church window. She prayed, recorded and explicated her visions, gave pastoral counseling, played with her cat, and presumably died a peaceful old woman, only to be reborn phoenix-like in these last decades as a kind of Queen of Women's Consciousness. She lived through three outbreaks of plague, the Great Schism, the Peasants' Revolt, and various miseries generated by worse-than-usual monarchs, and yet her favorite word is bliss. Fascinated by intellectual history, I wonder, but will never know, what had prepared Julian to write in her Middle English that God "enioyeth" being our father, our mother and our spouse? She wrote of the Trinity as maker, keeper and lover. In a century renowned for its images of hell, when purgatory was more significant than earth, what had planted in her soul that "al shal be wel, and al shal be wel, and al manner of thyng shal be wele"?[11] She claims that God told her. I do not know if ideas come like that, messages from the divine. At any rate, the visions did not trickle down the chain. The Trinity was in her.

Mostly these days Julian is honored for her revelation of God as Mother. Can we assume Julian was herself a mother, of children now dead, or unwilling to keep her, that she wrote so perceptively, without idealism, about childbirth and nursing? Medieval folk, you know, thought that breast milk was menstrual blood somehow reconstituted, as though in lactating women the monthly flow backed up, changed color, and poured out sweet. So it was that Julian could link birth blood, mother's milk, and the eucharist in such a wondrous way. Yes, sometimes ignorance does come in handy. Julian reigns now in the "God as mother" chapters of many recent books, and many feminist Christians, sick of God as father, are popularizing God as mother. And I say, cheers and beware. Cheers, that God is other than a narrow tradition, bigger than an old image, imaged also as a woman's being and body, and I have memorized "Mothering God," a hymn newly adapted from Julian's writings.

But I cannot cheer unreservedly. In a time of artificial insemination, in a society condoning single motherhood, we can become accustomed to the idea that the mother is the better or even the sole parent, a notion as wrongheaded as Aristotle's. During the nineteenth century, responsibility for the children switched from the father to the mother, and as a mother I am mightily weary of both those who romanticize mothering and those who blame their mothers for all the errors of their life. We must beware lest by sanctifying a metaphor we legitimate social, psychological, and ethical positions we would chose not to perpetuate. "Mother" is not a univocal symbol of goodness. "Mother" cannot include all women. (Let's list some women of renown: Hilda of Whitby, Gertrude of Helfta, Hildegard of Bingen, Catherine of Siena, Teresa of Avila, Jane Austen, George Eliot, Charlotte Bronte, Rebecca Jackson, Emily Dickinson, Louisa May Alcott, Sarah Orne Jewett, Katherine Anne Porter, Katharine Drexel, Edith Wharton, Flannery O'Connor: not a one bore children, and not all were the motherly sort.) We can decapitate fathers only to idolize mothers, and it is possible that our last state will be, at least psychologically, worse than our first.

For Julian, God's incarnation in Christ was God's connection with the human, God's embodiment into our pain. Because Jesus had a body which bled and suffered, just as women's bodies do, in Christ God became like a woman. This syllogism—Jesus suffered, women suffer, in Jesus God is like women—is both good news and bad news. I grin with glee that this woman wrote confidently of bliss in God's mercy during a century plagued by terror of God's judgment, and I am delighted that she boldly described God as female. But for me, entering the twenty-first century, woman is not all bleeding and suffering. As a minimizer, I see that also men bleed and suffer, some men more than some women. I do not want women to claim power out of a mythic store of female weakness. But looking back at Julian, I can be amazed at what she saw—though I cannot see it that way. I can admire what I must lay aside.

Genius notwithstanding, Julian was also a woman of her century. Wow, exclaim my students, she lived alone in a hut next to a church? Well, so did dozens of others. We know of over forty anchorholds in medieval Norwich alone. And I want to know the story of each Esmerelda. Was she old? mad? pregnant? dedicated to God? escaping some sorrow? But each has gone into her own mystery.

In another way Julian echoes her century. She chose pain, running toward it and grabbing on to it for dear life, as though in embracing suffering she was most closely connected to Christ, the Sufferer, whose suffering connected her with God. Our culture calls back to the medievals, You'd better see a therapist, get yourself into a twelve-step program, wing your way to happiness! But at a time when women had no control, or distressingly little, over their social status, income, husband, or pregnancies, when physicians were as likely to kill as to cure—you're feeling sick? let me bleed you—the joyous freedom to meet suffering head-on, rather than a futile effort to escape it, may have symbolized salvation. If you can't beat it, join it, and you might as well pack God along for the ride. But when I encounter in the contemporary world someone clutching on to pain, trying to suck life from death—I think of Thérèse of Lisieux—I am disgusted.

But my favorite image from Julian has to do with clothes.

One of the many topics touched on in Genesis 3 is clothing. The story of the human fall, although deeply disquieting in several ways, is a brilliantly insightful description of the awakening of human consciousness. We are innocent animals no longer. We have acquired a glorious and terrible knowledge of the self. We know of our failures, our sexual vulnerability, perhaps even our death, perhaps also of God. We look into each other's eyes, and we see mirrored there our own needy body. And so we find some fig leaves to cover ourselves up. We are glad for a buffer between ourselves and the frightening power of all that is not ourselves. But in this story God does not strip us bare and laugh at our shivering selves. Rather, mercifully, this God offers us sturdier clothing, waterproof, rip-proof, warm. The Baptist preacher said that God's compassion for the first couple occasioned the earth's first death, animals killed for their skins, they died so the man and the woman could survive.

As in most societies, our clothes protect us from weather, grant us sexual privacy, indicate our socio-economic status, bond us with others who dress similarly. Especially in our culture, clothes parade our individuality. My daughters told me they will inscribe on my tombstone "She Matched." For I much enjoy the play of clothing, the hobby of acquiring clothes at clearance sales in outlet stores, the daily mix-and-match of simple top, plain skirt and uncommon necklace. For years I watched with fascination the ingenuity of the girls who found countless ways to alter their required school uniforms into creative manifestations of self-expression, while still avoiding a detention for breaking the dress code. Yet our prized individuality is part mask. Not unlike the whalebone corsets you can try on at the Smithsonian Institution—and experience in an instant, by trying to take a deep breath, why all those nineteenth-century women spent their days fainting— my clothes hold me in, shape me, form me into the me that I want you to see.

But back to Julian. Precious few clothes she must have had there in her hut: what, two shifts, two gowns and one wool cloak? And so we're not surprised that she writes of God as her clothing, wrapping her in love. God as our Clothing: as if God both protects us from nature and shields us from one another's critical eyes; as if God were what encloses us as we face the world by day and admit to death each night. I think of my silk rebozo, several feet longer than other shawls. It wraps me up in heat or cold, its elaborate trim and flowing fringe making exquisite anything underneath: God as my silk rebozo.

But Julian wrote something more surprising. She wrote that in the incarnation God became "unornely clad." Having donned human nature, God now wore Adam's tunic, tight, short, and soiled. But now in the Trinity, Christ is "recheley clad in blissfull largess, and we be his corone. This was a singular mervel and a full delectable beholdyng, that we be his corone."[12] Julian has reversed the image, as genius writers do. Julian, our earliest extant female author of the English language, writes that Christ is wearing us. We are his crown. Julian writes that she is laughing aloud: God as our clothing and we as Christ's crown. Thanks to us, God gleams.

Learning from Julian to think always in threes, we give our imagery for God the Trinity-test. God our Clothing: first, our God is outside of us, encircling us, being the protection and warmth without which we cannot survive; second, our God donned human life in Jesus, who became the stuff of the earth and wore holes in himself in service to others, and when he needed it no longer, his seamless tunic was claimed by a Roman soldier; third, our God is vested by the community, seen in our baptismal gowns and albs, in our clothing drives, perhaps even our Easter hats. Julian's Trinity is a God who embraces the other, who becomes the other, and who is shared with the other. God our Clothing: it's a God a feminist could love.

our Sovereign Love

Two images of the divine were much used—overused?—in medieval Christianity: God the almighty king and God the passionate lover. I will endeavor a postmortem.

"King" was the more commonplace image, the public symbol for Christendom. King was about God's rule over the world and the church. King was about divine power of order, justice and, it was hoped, mercy. The image of king sat well with those European monarchs attempting to conquer first the Mediterranean world, then the globe, for those petty rulers could convince themselves that they were aspiring to godly obligations. From the fourth century onward, court rituals such as bowing and incensing entered an increasingly formalized liturgy. Court rhetoric—O Emperor, who has listened to us in the past, now grant this our humble petition—dictated the prose style of Western liturgical prayer. Churches came to look like throne rooms, the eucharistic table like a royal dias. A hierarchy of saints and angels took their allotted places between us down here and God's palace in the skies. Don't bother the king with that trivial request, minion; take it to a lower official of the court: how about St. Jude? Protestants continued to glorify the monarchy in their worship tradition. I cannot guess how many "Come Thou, Almighty King" hymns I know by heart.

"Lover" was the choice of the mystics, the private symbol of the dedicated believer. Lover was about God's reigning within the soul. Lover was about divine compassion, about God's loving us all the way to death, Christ's death, my death. It seems that the celibates, their virginal life affording no opportunity for enacted passion, did not let the language of sexual ecstasy lie dormant, but turned their reveries toward God. Especially after the turn of the millennium, both female and male mystics generated meditations, poems, and spiritual autobiographies that proclaimed the passionate love they shared with God. Bernard of Clairvaux wrote eighty-six lengthy sermons on the Song of Songs. The goal was spiritual union. We call the emotional adventures of Catherine of Siena and Teresa of Avila mystical marriages. Also this tradition comes down into Reformation hymnody. As "Jesus, priceless treasure" has it, "In thine arm I rest me." I recall that the two masterpieces of hymnody we call the King and Queen of Chorales—"Wake awake" and "O Morning Star," written by Phillip Nicolai, an unmarried Lutheran pastor—both incorporate the imagery of our marriage to God.

I think of T. S. Eliot's poem "Journey of the Magi"; the wise travelers had come to Bethlehem thinking that birth and death were different. Well, I thought kings and lovers were different, that God as lover corrected God as monarch. But as I study the mystics' passionate writing, I see that the two are one: the monarch all dressed up on a throne, the lover holding me in the night, both are my lord. Inspired by the erotic poetry of the Song of Songs, which was thought to be about King Solomon and his love, the genre blended monarchical and sexual imagery. "King" is about a command for the submission of the community, "lover" is about the joy of the submission of the soul. These lovers, God and the soul, were never construed as equals: God is the male half, and thus the dominant one whose body I joyously kiss and reverently embrace. Both images depict me as subservient under God.

A quotation from Mechthild of Magdeburg, a thirteenth-century German Beguine: "When the needy soul comes to the court, she is judicious and refined. She gazes at her God in high spirits. Oh, how tenderly she is welcomed there! She remains silent, longing boundlessly for his praise. With great longing he reveals to her his divine heart. ... When the exalted Sovereign and the little waif thus embrace and are united as water and wine, she turns to nothing and is transported out of herself. ... Then she says, 'Lord, you are my lover, my desire, my flowing fount, my sun, and I am your reflection.' This is the journey to court of a loving soul that cannot exist without God."[13] You see what I mean?

Item: That God is a male, and thus enjoys dominance over me, a female.

Item: That God is a king with power like a puppeteer over me, despite that as an American I fled monarchies and elect my own governance and judge bejeweled crowns to be the brain-crushers they often were.

Item: That "he" as lover is activity to my passivity, that this is no love between equals, that my ecstasy lies in my submission, ah, beat me, beat me!

Item: That the gist of these metaphors is the glorification of human weakness in the face of divine domination.

So what's a feminist to do with this broken record of subservience, subservience, subservience?

None of us knows whether there is a God, a being outside this created order, prior to life as we experience it, subsequent to our death and to the end of the universe. Were there such a being, it would be the ultimate reality. Often I think that there is not. But I choose to be a Christian. I elect to believe in such an ultimate reality. I accept that I am not God and that belief in the Trinity necessitates my walking differently than were there no such ultimate reality. Some people can walk well without a god: I desire to believe in such a God to assist my walking.

But before this deity I do not grovel, a helpless peon before a mighty monarch. God is not a queen whose orders I follow blindly. Am I to obey biblical injunctions? I realize that all those commandments heading in my direction come not directly from divine Sophia but filter through many folk whose wisdom quotient was not necessarily on the high side. Am I to heed an inner voice? I do not fantasize that my complex ambiguous unconscious is on any divine wavelength.

Ought I listen to the God of history? My reading of the past does not convince me that God is autocrat of the universe, dispensing good and ill in any discernable way. So I do not, like Esther, creep into the throne room. Rather, standing before God grants me the honor of my being. It heightens my sense of responsibility and inspires a straighter backbone. Thus God is not quite my king or queen.

"Lover" is not quite right either. The language of sexual passion should evoke intertwined equality, the yin and yang of shared balance, both participating in the other, each needing and completing the other, coextensive desire, parallel gift, always intense activity, throughout serene rest. Between God and me this cannot be.

But perhaps elided into Sovereign Love, the metaphors, reconstituted, will do. The realization that I am not sovereign is finally a gift to me. In life I need not rely on myself: something is greater. In death I need not fear oblivion: something is greater. Accepting that another is truly sovereign impels me to look beyond myself for indications of that other around me. My gaze goes from my own navel toward the Sovereign One, and as I search for the Sovereign One, I realize that the Sovereign One is in a world of others around me.

And if that Sovereign were Love? Not emotional highs—I was raised suspect of emotion—but each day, every year, one being with the other's being, overlooking the irritations, praising the other's excellences, surprising the other with gifts; not a love that conceals sorrow with laughter, but a love that accompanies us at work and play, at the dinnertable and the deathbed. This love is not the self-interest of a lord, but a perfected bond, beyond imagining, matchless, complete. It need not deprive the other to fill itself, for there has been created in the two the fullness of both.

So let's give "Sovereign Love" the Trinity-test. If God is the Sovereign who is fully Love, we see why God creates us as creatures capable of love; we honor Christ who exemplified love; and we join in God's community in which love hopes to reign.

Sovereign Love is something of what I mean by "God."

our Waiter, Winter, Weapon, whatever

Waiter: one who serves, not "Hi-I'm-Suzie-I'm-your-server," but black suit, elegant restaurant, silently, unobtrusively, anticipating desires, meeting needs: God as waiter

Washerwoman: a woman whose occupation is scrubbing recurring stains out of our sweaty clothes and our used sheets and our bloody towels: God as washerwoman

Witch: one who with thoroughgoing knowledge of the forces of nature, the habits of creatures, and the patterns in plants has power to change what is to what is better: God as witch

Wrestler: one who fought with Jacob long ago and with whom we contend still today, who at the end, after dislocating our limbs from their sockets, blesses us: God as wrestler

Winter: a period of dormancy, appearing lifeless but nurturing renewal: God as winter

Word: waves of sound connecting you and me, conveying part of myself to you; an I-love-you in the ear in the night: God as word

Whaleboat: the rowboat in which we venture out to harpoon the whale, because we need oil for our lamps; a craft well designed to keep us afloat in dangerously high seas: God as whaleboat

Wine: the centuries' old roots, the vine, the grapes, the juice, the chemical transformation, and finally the wine that gladdens the heart, lightens the mind, and unites the people at a table for two or a festival for many: God as wine

Wigwam: a circular family dwelling made of wooden poles and animal skins, handy for nomads to cart along as they travel: God as wigwam

Womb: the dark warm matrix within which we curl up and grow; our seedpod, our sleeping bag: God as womb

Watchtower: a phallic structure built on the edge of the city from which the sentries can spot the approaching enemy army: God as watchtower

Woodworker: one who carves and whittles, measures and polishes, recreating trees into chairs and tables, beds and bookshelves, refashioning woodlands into wood for us: God as woodworker

Wisdom: the goddess from ancient times who oversees the universe with justice and as tree of life offers superlative fruits for us to enjoy: God as wisdom

Weapon: any of many devices which protect me from harm by destroying it: God as weapon

Way: Confucianism teaches that the way is straight and hierarchical, Taoism observes that the way meanders through the forest—which is it? God as way

Whirlwind: wind turned wild, nature become preternatural, tearing Elijah away from Elisha and into heaven: God as whirlwind

Wall: it keeps our snarling dog from attacking the neighbors: God as wall

Wildfire: conflagration beyond comprehension; not as in the burning bush, a fire alive but not consuming, but blaze gone berserk—what's the purpose behind this uncontrolled destruction? God as wildfire

Water: that which extinguishes fire; one of those precious few things without which humans cannot long survive: God as water

Winding sheet: swaddling clothes for a corpse, wrapping me round at death, keeping me together even then: God as winding sheet

You stutter, looking for which w-w-words can begin to say God.

yes and no to each

I f you haven't seen the movie *A Month in the Country*, go rent it tonight. Two shellshocked World War I veterans are gradually recovering their sanity by uncovering some religious symbols from the past: the archeologist is digging for a buried Saxon church, and the art restorer is removing the whitewash in a Yorkshire church to reveal the fifteenth-century wall paintings that graced its interior until the Puritans whited them out. The parish's cold and nasty rector does not approve of this restoration project. He desires the parishioners' total attention to his sermons, and from his Slough of Despond he says of the mural, "It will distract." Behold another John Calvin, who enforced focus on himself, shrunk the people's religious imagination, prescribed one narrow way to God, until there is nothing between me and God but one black-robed male.

The Christian church has said yes to Father, Son, Spirit. Some Christians have said yes to Sovereign, Lover, Mother, Wisdom, and Way. Most would say no to Witch and Wigwam. I say yes and no to each. I will consider every new proposal, weighing its insight against the tradition. Each might capture something of mystery; yet any can become a black-robed male if it stands alone. The gem has many facets, and light must reflect off each for the jewel to shine.

The church interior of my childhood offered a single ill-conceived depiction of the Trinity for our perpetual meditation. The church of my teenage years, thoughtlessly copying the New England Protestant heritage, was colonial in design, and thus empty of imagery. But we crave images of grace, diverse pictures, all around us, one for this Sunday, one for next, yes and no to each, both cross and tree. And so also the congregation that worshipped in New York City's famous St. Peter's—as stark a vacuum of white and butcher block as a Quaker might admire—became hungry for images and came close to installing an abstract expressionist triptych by Willem de Kooning in a reckless search for something to fill the void. And I thought, oh boy, we could have three huge splashy colorful canvases set up before us as the black-robed male we adore.

I have traveled to churches with abundant images. And I do not mean only Chartres, with its brilliant glass so high up that, even wearing my thick glasses and consulting the guidebook, I can scarcely decipher the figures. No, I mean the village church in Pickering, England, where, as in the movie, the whitewash has been removed to reveal biblical sequences and saints' lives, and there in the crossing are some fetching demons boiling a cardinal in a cauldron in hell.

I mean the churches along the route running northwest from Stockholm, Sweden, with their interiors painted by Albertus Pictor, every inch of the walls and ceiling, dozens of Bible stories interlaced with vines and flowers, interspersed with adorable monsters and fanciful critters, even a bare-breasted mermaid looking down at the priest, and in the narthex the devil trying to chop down the tree of life. I mean the wooden church painted in 1490 by Master Armund: when the prodigal son returns home, his mother the Queen dresses him in a royal red robe. In several medieval churches in Finland, one reads the walls like salvation's book, first, to the right of the altar, the creation—with a mermaid in Eden's pond— then the fall, then a Jesse tree, then the annunciation and Christ's birth, all around the room until, at the left of the altar, heaven at the end of time. On the pillars are the saints. In San Vitale in Ravenna, Italy, are spectacular mosaics depicting the biblical narratives that are cited in the liturgy. Each image presents itself and distracts us from the others. We look at one, at another. We rock in the nave between salt waves on both sides.

Ah, but who gets to decide on which artist? Albertus Pictor: yes, Michelangelo: no; Chagall: yes, de Kooning: no. What?! You don't agree?

Church quarrels these days are often about the metaphors for God in hymn texts and prayers. Some Christians find comfort in one or few images, loving the familiar and hoping to keep at least religion changeless. Culture is the enemy, say some conservative theologians. Well, I say, some culture, yes: how about a little nuance here? Why would we assume that the Spirit of God is not helping to shape our culture? Perhaps, impatient with a moribund church, God is renewing the world in other ways. The church need not be a grand deep freeze, preventing rot by prohibiting the possibility of any new life at all, numbing our limbs and arresting our brains in the hope that nothing untoward may grow.

I do not claim that all images are equally appropriate. In fact, I led the charge against the de Kooning triptych, arguing that our congregation's task, far more difficult than convincing everyone to admire the red curves, was to find contemporary art that was both Christian in orientation and liturgical in intent. Nor do I suggest a quota system of divine images: one chosen by the theologians, one by the teenagers, one by women, one by men. I mean, rather, that we be inspired by the brilliant prayers penned by Thomas Cranmer in the sixteenth century. He offered doublets: almighty and merciful, honor and glory, help and goodness, righteousness and holiness, to think and to do. The speech is slower than colloquial English, but fitting as diction for prayer: one can rest in the space between the synonyms. Each smiles across the mystery at the other.

We commonly use the phrase "image of God" to mean a metaphor used to describe the divine, for example, when we cite water as an image of God. However, the phrase "image of God" as it appears in Genesis 1 means the opposite: not the way we imagine God, but how God was before humans existed and the godly design according to which our imaginations were formed. We are in God's image, rather than God in one of ours.

At their best, both Judaism and Christianity taught that since God is incorporeal, the divine image that Genesis cites cannot refer to anything physical. The medieval theologians reasoned that this image must be reason itself, that human quality most valued by the men who claimed that they had more of it than women. From this imagined male characteristic was constructed an image of God which then God returned back to earth as the very image in which males had been created. Just a tad circular in thought? It is understandable that many feminists now urge that God be described as female, so that also women can know themselves to be created in the divine image. Yet in parallel fashion to the logic of the Middle Ages, since God is believed to be beyond body, we must now scramble to suggest what it is about femaleness that is particularly divine. And as for the metaphor of God's womb: let's admit that not even the most hardened Christian androcentrists ever talked in the liturgy about God's penis.

It will take, what, a century before the churches experience a healthy multiplicity of images for God? One sees the creativity most clearly now in new hymnody—the dozens of recent hymn texts exuberant with innovative images of God. The task of normalizing the proliferation of divine images is so monumentally massive that I should be content merely to help push this boulder up the side of the mountain.

But I hope for the century beyond that. I hope for the time when, beyond the male theologians lecturing on God as father and the women's groups praising God as mother, each sees God in the other, as the other. I hope for the time that God need not be like me—it's always handy to have God resemble me—but God is like the other, and I am drawn to that other as a necessary part of the I-who-I-are.

Yes, I hope for the time when divine images, already having confirmed the confident self, can affirm the distant other. I want my images of God to include the part of me that lives in Africa, the part of me that wrote the Nicene Creed, the part of me starving herself in a medieval convent, both the part of me excited by the government's offer of 640 acres for homesteaders and the part of me paralyzed at the thought of the westward trek away from parents and family and friends.

So I walk in the boundary between the medieval God and the postmodern God. You need sturdy shoes: it's an uneven path. And indeed, sometimes in the middle of a Sunday liturgy, you have to say no. You close the hymnal, or you belt out altered words, or you seal yourself off and memorize an inclusive language translation of a psalm. When I was in elementary school, my family attended a Community Concert performance of Handel's Messiah. We had front row balcony seats. At the Hallelujah Chorus everyone dutifully arose—except my father, who later explained he didn't see any reason to stand up for some piece of music just because a British king had done so. And when I refuse to sing a hymn, I recall how mortified I was at my dad's resistance, and I smile.

is God for us

ere's a commonplace American deity: God-for-me. In this religion, the Christian teaching of the consummate value of each individual before God has elbowed out anything that could relativize the grand Me. I have a divine core—my immortal soul—and a divine destiny—heaven. God loves me ultimately. I can channel divine assistance when I need it, perhaps for a heart by-pass or a teenager in trouble; omnipotence is on call and will be at my side momentarily. God's power is understood primarily if not solely as an antidote to the poisons in my life. I need not participate in any religious tradition, which would lay on me unnecessary and burdensome obligations, for all that matters is the transcendental couple: God and me.

If God is for-me, I am like Odysseus with Athena. I'm her special boy, and her power is on my side. Indeed, I'm far luckier than Odysseus because since my God is the only God around, I don't have to contend with angry Poseidon who is planning to swamp my ship. Because Americans value individual liberty above nearly anything else, we give this religion a lot of slack. News commentators speak respectfully of even religion gone psychotic, leery of criticizing anybody's God-for-me. If that's your God, well, go for it. At least you'll be happy on your journey home from Troy.

Here's a second popular American deity: God-apart. This is the God of Aristotle, of Benjamin Franklin, the scientific Prime Mover that brilliantly began creation but hasn't done much since. God exists in a pure realm of god-ness that is unrelated to human life. God reigns in monarchical splendor over, actually, nothing: the created order is not subject to God, there is no value in praying, God is not the type of primordial power that cares whether my daughters get home safely at night. Oh, Franklin was all for religion, donating towards many Philadelphia churches, for he reasoned that the practice of religion was good for those who needed it, who hadn't been educated into the God-apart. As Albert Einstein said, a personal God, a God-for-me, is a childish, even selfish malformation of religion. Religion, Einstein claimed, must be the human search for the moral life. A being called God doesn't have much if anything to do with it.

Americans, the pollsters report, are keen on God even if God cannot be expected to do very much. In Europe, people who have discarded God-for-me tend to dump the deity altogether. A true secularist doesn't keep God-apart around for long. God-apart is the bizarre antique vase on the top shelf that we'll never use. Besides, it leaks. Get rid of it at the next yard sale. If God is apart, let God go. Cut the tether. God will float off into space like a casualty in a science fiction movie, never to show up in the script again.

In my version of religion, God is God-for-us.

(Granted that my mind usually reasons that there probably is no god. Granted that immature, even distasteful, depictions of God are evident Sunday after Sunday to any critical observer. Granted, that when one wonders what God is, the images that jump to mind are piteously inadequate. What comes up on your screen? Michelangelo's middle-aged creative man, which is, of course, a grandiose image of Michelangelo himself; a sentimentalized Jesus wearing a robe and walking by my side; a primordial womb in which the entire universe swims; perhaps a force in a Star Trek-like parallel reality that intersects with ours on rare occasion. None of these images is profound enough. Even my beloved tree of life is wholly insufficient as an image of ultimate reality.)

So rejecting both God-fór-me as a child's birthday party and God-apart as an antiseptic idea, how can I imagine God-for-us? I was told of an educated Hindu woman listening to a temple lecturer who said that all misfortune arises solely and inevitably from our misbehavior. She asked, in sorrow and disbelief: could all the misery in Africa be the result of karma? (The lecturer remonstrated: this is a bad question.) Our minds try to grasp the magnitude of human suffering, and the torrent of wretchedness washes away our hopes to provide a solution. We can't imagine a deity qualified enough to fill the job description. So it is easy to find ourselves settling for Favorite Aunt (God-for-me) or Retired Chief of Staff (God-apart). All this I know. But I try.

I can say it this way: I would sooner live believing in God than not. And if God is about ultimate reality, it couldn't be narrowly for me. God will have to be that which connects me to the other and so be God-for-us. I have lived my life within a community of believers. Although through half a century the church has bulldozed lots of trash in my direction, I—with most of my family and many of my friends—have together climbed right through it and are heading down the road. While we plod along, we tell each other stories of other plodders, folks from the Bible and out of history who encountered what they described as divine mercy, and we identify with the characters in these stories. Their tales of sorrow and salvation became ours. We joined the us that God is for.

To illustrate the deity as God-for-us, Christian theologians have retold the story of God's visit to Abraham and Sarah. According to Genesis 18, the couple is old and childless: "it had ceased to be with Sarah after the manner of women." Three visitors arrive at Abraham's tents, pitched at an oasis by an oak grove. Sarah and Abraham serve them a meal, and the three, suddenly speaking as if they are one, promise Sarah a son. Christians, who during their early centuries retained from Judaism a prohibition against sculpting God as a bull or a Zeus, were drawn to this elusive tale: the three visitors who are one visitor are/is God promising life to Sarah and to us.

The Eastern church came to revere icons of this story. Most of the icons show three beings at a laden table, both Abraham and Sarah serving, their house and oak grove in the background. But in the fifteenth century the genius Andrew Rublev distilled this image down to its theological essence: the grove became a single tree, the feast a single chalice; Abraham and Sarah have been replaced by the viewers, who are drawn by the circular force of the icon's lines to join the three at the table.

There are many reasons why this icon beckons me. It recalls an ancient Jewish memory of a theophany. It depicts one God as three united asexual presences. Because their eyes look at one another, at the cup, and at our place at table, we are pulled toward the table to God. The chalice evokes the Sunday liturgy. The icon juxtaposes Abraham's solid house with the ethereal nimbuses of the visitors. And there is a tree.

A Trinity could be neither God-for-me nor God-apart. The threeness of this deity means that not even God's self is a monad apart but requires the circle of three to be one. The chalice of the Rublev icon is so massive a loving cup that surely it is not meant that I drink alone. The others will share the cup with me. The single-swallow shot glasses prefilled with wine that one encounters at some communion services these days are an American God-for-me invention that shrinks the communal largess into a dose of medicine for me: one tablespoonful once a week, and my devil will vanish. Rather, the point of God-for-us is that my access to God is communal, my reception of God is communal, my participation in the divine life is communal. A jigger doesn't do it.

Here's one more story for the trek: It's as if we all, everyone we know, and at the last everyone who has ever lived, are Noah's family and the animals. We live nearly overwhelmed by disaster. But we also see evidence of the mercy of God: over all is the rainbow, and under our feet the wood of the ark, and alighting on our hands the dove of peace. In the name of God, the Rainbow, the Ark, the Dove, we and all the other animals sail on.

The image isn't perfect, but, I think, better than Michelangelo's.

even feminists are in need

T here are so many ways to be needy, unique ways, private ways, run-of-the-mill ways, universal ways.

Early Christian theologians sought to convince the world that all humans needed God. We read a second-century apologist explaining that Christians always thanked God for their food: we need food, God provides it, and the faithful ought to acknowledge this need of God's goodness. But it wasn't food that preachers focused on, perhaps because then, as now, most of the people listening were not desperately hungry. It was divine forgiveness that theologians said was our primary need.

That I am at fault is a classic Western conviction. Oedipus is searching for the culprit who turns out to be himself. The idea that the primary human problem is infraction against God's will became a dominant Jewish idea after the Babylonian victory over Jerusalem, the destruction of the temple, and the deportation of the conquered elite from the land to enemy territory. The Hebrew people had believed that God's part of the covenant was to protect the nation. The cataclysm of the exile sent devout minds scrambling: well, they concluded, we must have sinned, and in a big way, for it isn't God's nature to allow such disaster willy-nilly. And so we read Psalm 51, supposedly the plea of King David after his adultery with Bathsheba and the murder of Uriah have been found out: "Have mercy upon me, O God . . . blot out my transgressions." However, if you read the entire psalm, you'll discover what this lament is really about: "Rebuild the walls of Jerusalem." Clearly the psalm was composed not by David in 1000 B.C.E., but by the exiles in 500 B.C.E, the agonized writer confessing that it must be my sins that brought about the tragic destruction of God's holy city: Forgive me, O God.

At least, you must grant, they took morality seriously.

So sin as offense against God is even back then a second-level neediness. The first level of neediness is basic human survival: we need the sun, the rain, health, family, a homeland. With God on our side, we are promised that these needs will be met. But on top of this endless need yet another developed: I need forgiveness for having reneged on my part of the God-gives-graciously-and-I-act-righteously religious arrangement.

From this developed the notion of God as Nineteenth-Century-Primary-School-Teacher, God up in front of the classroom bellowing, "If you don't complete your memorization assignment, I'll take away your recess time." Human tragedy was understood largely as a punishment from God. Why is my child sick? I messed around as a teenager. How alive is this small, even solipsistic view of God? At least in my circles, such a punitive divine law-giver is already moribund, the bones of this malevolent deity available for viewing in any good theological library. But undoubtedly I am naive, hoping that this God is dead. Perhaps this God is shouted out and bargained with each Sunday around the world.

But agreeing that God is not Charles Dickens' Mr. Gradgrind does not answer whether forgiveness is our pressing need. Let me tell you what I hear from my students. To insure against plagiarism, I generally require that student papers, of which I read about eight hundred a year, include personal reflection. From this continuous source of student opinion I have learned that, while nearly all my students identify themselves as Roman Catholic, they are similar to their religious and nonreligious counterparts in colleges throughout the country, more formed by mass media than by the medium of the mass. As young Americans, they are not into sin. Most shrug off original sin, as having been washed away at their infant baptism, and many reject sinful nature, viewing everyone but serial killers as basically good. Sin has been replaced by mistakes, occasional screw-ups, growth experiences.

Once I asked, was a first grader who swatted a friend sinning? No, they said. A sixth grader? No. Well, when would you call it sin? One eighteen-year-old called out, "At twenty-one." They find the idea that human will is headed in a wrong direction as demeaning, archaic, akin to burning witches and impaling heads on poles at the city gates. Some judge all this sin-talk as a futile attempt to render them ashamed for harmless sexual activity. In a class discussion of Genesis 3, one student expressed disgust at the expulsion from the garden: why didn't God just forgive the couple? I think of the story in John 8, Jesus saying to the woman taken in adultery, "Sin no more." Our society has rearranged the words: "No more sin."

Feminist theologians have presented a no more acquiescent critique of the traditional teaching about sin. To the church's obsession with perpetual personal failings many feminists have said, Why don't you speak for yourself, John? O'erweening ego as the root cause of selfish pride is, yes, a man's problem. But a woman's problem is the Doormat Syndrome: here, I'm nothing, let me lie down before you, please wipe your dirty feet on me. As nineteenth-century Elizabeth Cady Stanton called out, women need more ego, not less. Paul, Augustine, Luther: these were males in midlife crises, and their analyses of their lives do not fit women's experience. Let men attack their own egomania, but leave us to develop ourselves. The sin that many feminists focus on is the system of oppression which has been created and maintained largely by men.

How can we know to what degree women are still reared to be doormats? Before Charlotte Bronte focused herself on creating *Jane Eyre,* while the aimless life in the small town of Haworth was unhinging at least her emotions, she wrote to a dear friend the nineteenth-century female credo: "The right path is that which necessitates the greatest self-sacrifice—which implies the greatest good to others."[14] How many American women would say such a thing now? The women I associate with are everything but doormats, the women I teach more ambitious for individual success than the men in class. Although cemeteries are full of them, I don't run across many women lying around embalmed by self-sacrifice. Rather, I encounter women identifying sin as a system outside themselves and claiming that their primary sin would be to deny their potential.

As with other topics, in this I am a minimizer. Of course, some women were raised to be flattened as doormats. I think of my mother who over the decades has nursed six dying people, cheerfully accomplishing the daily unpleasant tasks required, finding her fulfillment in serving others. But as most feminists now admit, there is no universal woman's experience that makes me similar to my mother. My temptation is not to lie down to be walked on, but to attain to that pedestal that you see through the archway at the museum. Look at me, a new David in the Gallery in Florence! Yet I reject the suggestion that this predisposition makes me less of a woman. Women and men: both can cast themselves as doormats or aspire to exquisite statuary. To make too much of a sex-bound distinction diminishes human complexity and trivializes cultural contexts. All us women publishing memoirs: if such books are not pedestal monuments, I do not know what they are. And to publish a book which says "I am nothing" is self-deception beyond belief.

I do not know whether I am trapped by my formation. As a child I was dished up lots of sin, and as a teenager I dutifully read a set of questions and answers from my catechism before going to communion services: "Do you believe that you are a sinner? Yes, I believe it; I am a sinner." But whether because of mind-numbing repetition or by accurate observation, I continue to believe that the human will is inherently ill-directed. To think this out we need not reconstruct some "fall." We know that humans were not at the first demigods, immortal and sinless. Indeed, I accept that we evolved from other animals that also must attend to both preservation of the self and commitment to the species. But inevitably, it seems to me, we humans find these dual responsibilities impossible to balance: we turn against others—the egocentric motif—or against ourself—the doormat syndrome. A wholly whole and healthy I: it does not ever occur. And I'd like a more profound theory than that people had bad mommies—an explanation that loses its appeal in the delivery room—or that the mistake wasn't that bad anyway.

But beyond pedestals or doormats: Much that grows worthy or wonderful if not kept in check can take over the garden. When I hear of women presenting their newly-bleeding thirteen-year-old daughters with moon jewelry, I am glad. I did the same. But not all bleeding is healthy. I remember as a young teenager lying in bed with my posterior raised high and the pediatrician trying to think of some way to stop my six weeks of continuous bleeding. In those antediluvian pre-hormone days, he suggested breaking my hymen: since married women had fewer menstrual irregularities than single women, well, breaking my hymen seemed like a quick fix. Fortunately, my bleeding stopped on its own. But countless other times, life became death, the bleeding emptying out women completely. Of my great-great-great-grandfather's four wives, two died with their infants in childbirth. Only adolescents imagine life without limits, growth without cancer, nature without neediness.

A partial list of feminist neediness:

— food, not too much, not too little
— milk for the babies
— a place to bury the dead: wastebaskets won't do
— to endure the chemotherapy and radiation
— not to be raped
— not to be walked on
— forgiveness for walking on others
— a community
— for your children to come home safely at night
— to vault over walls wrongly erected
— to accept those limits that belong to humankind
— an answer or two
— the peace that passes understanding
— for someone to hold you as you are dying

— wisdom: Should I euthanize my cat? My vet agreed, it was time, Pinny was seriously disturbed, there is no Valium Spray for such as my poor pet. But even in this small ethical decision, I knew my neediness: I was to kill this cat, baptized several times by my daughters years ago—"She is now a cat of God," one had said. I wanted in that office not only me and pitiful Pinny and the compassionate vet Carolyn: I wanted a magnificent figure whose wisdom towered above us, ordering the natural world into a heaven, protecting us from chaos as we willed death. I needed wisdom.

Lots of neediness.

of what Christ might mean

C hrist is like the Christmas tree: available in several basic styles and countless individual renderings. There's the pre-decorated-flocked artificial
tree, the purist's white-star-real-candle tree, the kids'-art-projects-and-
popcorn tree. One January, putting away the Christmas decorations, I surrepti-
tiously retired the worst of the summer camp ornaments, and the next December
my teenage daughters, examining all the ornaments laid out on the sofa, called
out, "OK, so where's the seashell baby Jesus?"—which only demonstrates that
even our most enlightened attempts to trash the trash may meet with considerable
opposition. Many people like their old Jesus.

But others are pitching not only the worst Jesus ornaments but the entire
tree. That a man named Jesus lived in Palestine in the first century appears un-
deniably factual. But whether he merits an honorific, a religious metaphor, perhaps
even a divine title, is the point of contention, then as now. I want to think
through some images of Jesus, keeping one or two, repairing another, throwing
several out. But I am quite aware that after wrenching decades of personal and
religious upheaval, some feminists must clean house of Christs that I never had
around in the first place.

Take for example a Jesus-by-my-side piety. Many Protestant women were
taught to trust an omnipresent man who walked at their side through the dark
streets, who stood guard at their bed keeping intruders away, who whispered
comfort in their ear. These women, who sang "Beautiful Savior" and "What a
Friend We Have in Jesus" weekly in their churches, are working now to excise this
man from their feminist consciousness. But my no-nonsense German ancestry
did not implant this silent and sweet Jesus into my brain, and thus I require no
surgery to remove him.

Feminists have rightly criticized the androcentric reading of the incarnation
that makes essential the maleness of Jesus; but at least a Jesus-by-my-side was not
very much like a man. Long gone is the explicit sexual imagination of the medieval
mystics, Margery Kempe wearing a wedding ring given her by Jesus and swooning
over handsome young men as reminders of her man Jesus. Or, as Hadewijch of

Brabant describes her participation in the sacrament, "And he came himself to me, took me entirely in his arms, and pressed me to him; and all my members felt his in full felicity, in accordance with the desire of my heart and my humanity."[15] No, most Jesus piety offered either an asexual being—as distant from vibrating sexuality as the virgin birth—or a somewhat effeminate character, who didn't work for a living and who sported long curls and a white robe. Indeed, recent study of early medieval iconography suggests that the depiction of Christ riding on a donkey was a deliberate attempt to feminize the image of Christ the conquering emperor, for a real man would ride a horse, never a donkey. The nineteenth-century fantasy of the natural female, all gentle nurturing of others, all passive suffering for others, provided a comforting frame for much Jesus piety, as Jesus became more a mother standing by my bed than a man lying in my bed or a father glimpsed in the doorway. (It is a great pity that American English has no noun to designate an adult child. Calling Jesus "son" of God accentuates his sex, calling Jesus "child" infantilizes him. Each language presents its own stumbling blocks to religious expression.)

Imagining Jesus as a man, whether babysitter or warrior, increases in proportion to our reading the Bible as history. The catechesis of my childhood sought to teach me the Jesus-of-history. Our religion wasn't based on myth, I was taught, but on history, and we tried to tap into the consciousness of the living Jesus. Sermons were time machines transporting us back to Jesus: what was he doing, thinking, feeling? The current three-year lectionary represents a more critical look at the Bible as history. Sometimes now one hears preachers comparing John's Jesus to Matthew's, Mark's, and Luke's, weighing each for its credibility and value.

Others besides preachers are searching for the historical Jesus both in and outside the Bible. There's the Jesus of the Q document, or the Jesus of the Jesus Seminar, or the Jesus of the early Christians' egalitarian community before the male chauvinists muscled the women out. For the scholars who propose these new—that is, original—Christs, the Bible is not inspired authority, but untrustworthy propaganda, an inaccurate distortion of history. I find, however, that most of the Jesus proposals look strangely like idealized composites of the preferences of the eager compilers.

But the church must move beyond both the popular piety of Jesus-by-my-side and the scholarly search for Jesus-of-history in order to approach Christology, the theological articulation of what Christ means to believers. The very word "Christology," utilizing the honorific Christ, asserts that the Jesus of imagination or history is not enough. Some feminist theology asserts that the church's "high" Christology got off the path; we're now on a side track heading to a storage shed; we must go back to the switch and get going another way. A high Christology describes Christ as God. Refusing to incorporate a male into God, these feminists prefer a "low" Christology. For them, Jesus is not divine, God not triune. Rather, Jesus shows us how to live. In seeking a just life, by urging change in a stifling society, Jesus suffered in life and death, as do countless women and men, and God suffers with Jesus and us. Strength and, it is hoped, victory come from living through the suffering. For all women who suffer, there is the hope of the resurrection.

However, the dominant Christology in the Western tradition was not Jesus-suffering-with-us, but Christ-suffering-for-us. In the twelfth century, Anselm proposed the substitutionary theory of atonement: God's justice demanded punishment for sin, and Jesus substituted for us, suffering for us, taking our punishment for us. This formulation rested on a medieval notion that fathers owned their sons. Thus a father giving up his son was a gift of the self, not, as contemporary people would see it, child abuse. Anselm's theory is repulsive to many feminists, who from the pain of their personal experience discredit any such praise of passive suffering. (To what extent is this theory still preached? We need not beat a skeleton. To the degree that this language is alive and well, the church is enervated.)

As with Jesus-by-my-side, Anselm's presentation of the acquiescent son of a juridical God was, thankfully, not a big part of my rearing. Oh, yes, I sang it in hymns in which God and Jesus are conversing about doctrinal details. But I never took the image to heart. Although I sang at night, "Lord Jesus, since you love me, now spread your wings above me," I never pictured either Jesus or God as a winged being. Some images stick, others don't.

For some Christians, Jesus was bleeding, bleeding for us, crucifixes all over the house, graphic, gory, even disgusting. Perhaps the medieval people who worshiped these open wounds were themselves immobilized by pain, both women and men nailed to the wall by disease with no medicine, labor with no vacation, marriage with no choice, subsistence food, death in childbirth. At least some of this focus on the bleeding body is perhaps the psychic task of midlife, the Pauls, Augustines, Francises, Luthers and Bonhoeffers among us who, foreseeing that their own death will come to bury their aspirations, saw in the death of a man who was raised to life an antidote to their angst. Even for Julian the bleeding Jesus was a symbol of life.

I can accept some degree of this, for it is neither true nor healthy for Americans to pretend that there is no death. But I cannot spend my days gazing at what is nothing more than a nearly naked man bleeding on a pole. The crucifixion must glimmer in the light. Like Wallace Stevens' poem about the blackbird, there must be "thirteen ways of looking at" the cross. On my wall is a crucifix depicting Jesus as a Haitian peasant nailed to the trunk of the tree of life, military tanks and soldiers in the background, ripe colorful fruits near his open palms.

The Christology important in my childhood was what theologians call the classical theory of atonement. It's imagery about the warfare between good and evil. According to this mythic presentation, God and the devil battle it out on Calvary; on Good Friday the devil assumes victory, but on Easter Day is surprised to find that Christ has won. It's Aslan coming back to life after the White Witch does him in on the stone table. Martin Luther liked the ruggedness of this imagery, and although some Lutheran theologians have adopted from the battle language an excessively pugnacious attitude which they apply to all their pursuits, attacking slightly different Lutherans as if they are the antichrist, the imagery has potential. Obviously metaphoric—Jesus was no warrior—it takes evil seriously and focuses not on passive suffering but on the mystery of the resurrection. The image also can engender self-confidence: just as God was in Christ conquering evil, so now God is in us, doing the same. I am Joan of Arc.

For some believers reared in a high Christology, notably Roman Catholics, the once and future Jesus is Sophia. Bible studies are newly attentive to the Jewish poems praising God's Lady Wisdom, who created the world, effects justice, and serves a banquet of bread and wine. The ancient female image got swamped by the male Christ, and women are pulling her back into the boat. Indeed, some eminent feminist theologians base considerable hope for Christian renewal in her reign. I am glad of her resuscitation. When in worship the lector completes the Bible reading, I like the response, "Holy Wisdom, holy Word: Thanks be to God." Here is no sappy mommy: this is Ms. Truth on the pedimental frieze of the court house. Wisdom is what we need, in the debate over abortion, in the agonies of divorce, in contemplating the use of our money, in rearing our children. In Sirach 24, Sophia is the tree of life, and we thrive on her life-giving fruit.

But Sophia cannot save the church. Her elevation is bittersweet, a retrieval of what was after all a poetic compensation within divine patriarchy. All the biblical Sophia texts combined, although stirring poetry, would fill only several pages, for even in her heyday she was a minor metaphor. I notice, ruefully, that Sophia is popular among especially Roman Catholic women whose rearing in Marian piety makes worship of a goddess second nature. And as a minimizer, I find any inference that women are wiser than men counterproductive for society, and probably untrue.

To this collection—gentle Jesus at my side, the elusive historical Jesus, Jesus oppressed and suffering with me, a bleeding Christ suffering for me, a victorious

Christ conquering the devil, magisterial Sophia herself—let me propose another: Jesus as the opening up of God. Here's how it goes:

Religion is not always evil or stupid, but it is always limited, by our minds, our vocabulary, our context, our experience. Thus repeatedly religion must be opened up, blossoming with more beauty into deeper truth. Think of the bhakti devotees reinterpreting the legends of Hinduism, or second-century Judaism spiritualizing ancient animal sacrifice. Our records of Jesus indicate that he kept opening up religion, by telling surprising stories, dismissing taboos, honoring the ordinary, breaking rules as the way toward greater commitment, reversing the natural progression of disease and death. Our religious packaging is always too constricted: Jesus says, open the box, open it up.

But most important: we had thought we knew who and where God is. Why, God is the law-giver way up above the mountain top, or God is our people's protector inhabiting the temple, or, now-a-days, God is my interior spiritual self. But the more our ancestors reflected on Jesus, the more they came to believe that God is also a person among us. God is connected to us by being one of us. Christology brings God out of the clouds, and outside my imagination. God has feet, not on a footstool in the sky, not on my neck, but dirty with the dust of the earth. Jesus made us see a new dimension of God. Jesus was the opening up, not only of religion, but also of God.

And what of Jesus "saving" me? From hell? Along with an increasing number of Christians, I do not believe that hell exists. There is no eternal pit of fire from which to be rescued. From punishment for sin here on earth? I see no evidence that God is busy meting out appropriate penalties—for each petty sin one disappointment, for each medium sin a one-day grief, for each super sin a tragedy. If we are saved from anything, it is from ourselves. I am freed from a life kept small and constricted—not to say boring—by continuous rotation around myself. I am released from the lie that I am the center of the world. I have been opened up. I have been given a meaning beyond myself. God's incarnation saves me from a monotheism of the self: by recognizing God in Jesus, I move my sights from the mirror to the other.

One last word on Jesus. I do not pretend to have the problems of Christology solved or to have satisfied all feminist Christians. But that my proposal is partial and only in process does not keep me from going to church. The opposite is the truth: perhaps next Sunday I'll come to see it better than today. There are endless pages in the book. The tree keeps growing.

and the Spirit give

od's third dimension is the Spirit. Many Christians are used to going up to God and over to Jesus, but are much less comfortable with going into the Spirit. Yet it is precisely this third dimension that gives feminist Christians the depth we need.

Rather than being blown by divine gusts into adventures of the Spirit, the church has tried over and over to bottle the Spirit up into a nice holy jar for its own private use. The precious Mason jar in the church of my childhood was labeled Doctrine. Carefully canned therein was all the truth of God, all that was needed for sharing in God's life. Doctrine was how God was manifested in the world: incredible, I know, but there it was. And of course, when you have God neatly contained, you didn't want to open things up, lest your own brilliant genie escape. Other churches have their own sacred casks: Church Hierarchy or Ethnic Tradition or Historic Ritual or Ecstatic Utterance or Individual Conversion Experience—each a somewhat small container within which God's Spirit is shelved in the church. It is easier to encase God's Spirit in some book and process around holding it high than to let the Spirit blow itself—and us—where it will.

As well, the images of the Spirit that the church displays are stunted. Banners hanging in our churches depict the fiery Spirit as a harmless felt flicker, as if the church were a fondue pot over the Spirit's tiny flame: nothing to be concerned about here. Baptismal fonts have shrunk from the rivers of the first century to the fingerbowls of the nineteenth: don't worry, you won't really get wet. And our representations of the Spirit as a dove can suggest a sentimental nursery ornament rather than the primordial miracle that, with the chaotic flood now over, God's Spirit is recreating the world.

But I hear an objection: isn't "spirituality" the latest buzz word at retreats and seminaries and chain bookstores? Yes, but often in a Henry David Thoreau sense, spirituality being the way an individual is religious, the technique I chose (honoring nature? writing journals? following Ignatius?) to access and express the holy. But since religion is meant to be a communal belief and a group value system, an

83

individual's spiritual lifestyle is itself only another blessed beaker, this time bottled up and drunk down by the self. One sign of alcoholism: drinking alone.

Here's what the Bible claims: the Spirit is the manifestation of a continuously creating God. The Spirit is that dimension of God described by religious visionaries and enacted by the human community. John's gospel—always several layers deeper than the other gospels—describes the Ascension and Pentecost by saying that on Easter evening Jesus breathed on his disciples and gave them peace. So on Sunday morning when Christians exchange the greeting of peace, they are not merely saying a good morning and conveying their own heightened—or depressed?—sense of well-being. The idea is that they are passing around God's Spirit of the resurrected Christ within the community, the Spirit who, as the Nicene creed says, is the giver of life. The Spirit is the animation that God breathed into humankind on creation day; the Spirit is the mystery of the resurrected Christ; and the Spirit is the future of God reshaping the community. And lest we think of the Spirit as the poor third cousin, trinitarian theologians have taught that the Spirit is co-equal with the Son and the Father.

As a kid I had a glow-in-the-dark plastic plaque that read "Jesus never changes." Well, he did, continuously, and one need only read the four gospels, or the texts of hymns composed over the centuries, to see that. But I think no one could suggest that the Spirit never changes. The life of the Spirit is always testing the waters: is the new harbor better than that old? Although the past has situated us where we are in the present, and wise persons like to know how they got where they are, our future with God is not bound by the outlines of past or present: surely this is one meaning of "the resurrection." Feminists need a Spirit with a track record of breaking down the historic categories of sacred and profane, for women know well the problems that come from being labeled profane. And perhaps we will discover that power in the Spirit need not be taken away from one group to be given to another: perhaps the divine Spirit can be creating always more life, with plenty of life to go around.

We are bound to recognize the Spirit when it shows up in a familiar outfit. Ah, that energetic hymnsinging—now, there's the Spirit! Mother Teresa's sisters finding dying babies in the city's morning trash—there's the Spirit! Especially evangelical Christians are caught up in Spirit talk. But to me, a northern European introvert, their God acts rather like a cheerleader at the kind of a summer camp volleyball game I avoid. And so the controversies continue: Is the classic liturgy or a brand new song-and-dance the best vehicle for the Spirit? Is apostolic succession a wholesome sign of the Spirit, or only more slag from patriarchy? (Those phallic miters: really now.) We don't agree which century and culture most closely embodied the Spirit's idea of communal ethics. Some of us look on strange and wondrous trees and find on them the fruits of the Spirit, but other Christians see there only some wretched weed, and they organize a brigade to uproot the pest.

I do not pretend that I alone can always correctly distinguish a weed from a rare sapling. I need to check out my judgment with others. The Spirit of God is only in a seriously limited way in me. The Spirit is rather in us, in me only to the extent that I am connected with the others in the circle. This third dimension of the divine does not make me, big little me, an incarnation of God; rather, it renders us, the community—some biblical passages suggest the whole creation—the third place where God is.

One of the quarrels between the Eastern and the Western churches is technically termed the *filioque* controversy. What it comes down to is this: does God's Spirit function only through Christ, that is, somehow solely in or through the church, or can we say that the life of trees is also a sign of God's Spirit? As a Western Christian I should lean toward the first, but I'm in the middle. I'd say it this way: the church is too small a flagon for the Spirit; of course God's life is also in the forest. However, the church receives the Spirit's life through Christ and has no particular expertise about divine life in trees. So, although the life of Christ on the cross is somehow also at one with the life of trees, we have more words about the cross. But let's not forget the trees.

The Quakers have shaped their weekly meeting to experience this Spirit of God. The room is devoid of images, which are judged more likely to impede than to assist communication with the Inner Light of God. The people face one another, since God is understood as residing within the community. Each individual can speak freely a personal insight, but the goal of the assembly is to discern the sense of the meeting, to participate in those convictions which the majority of Friends share. Thus, even in the highly individualistic piety of the Quakers, the Spirit in the self defers to the Spirit in the community.

Few churches that I have visited capture this Spirit in art. I think of the church of Saint Apollinaire Nuovo in Ravenna, Italy. The apse is plain, its art having been destroyed in an earthquake. But the nave's walls are flanked by magnificent mosaics, on the left the procession of female virgins and on the right the procession of male martyrs. Each martyr—hair, facial expression, the crown he carries—is different from his neighbor. But the virgins! Each of the twenty-two women is sumptuously arrayed: jewels in her hair, necklaces and bracelets and belts of brilliant color and design, each woman wearing a different brocade pattern in her robe, each carrying a unique crown. Yet the figures flow in unison as though drawn by an invisible force, gentle yet unfaltering. The grandeur of these processions, the force of their beauty, their exquisite majesty flanking our worship space, is one depiction of the Spirit, God not only up in heaven or on the cross but surrounding and infusing and transforming us as we stand together here to pray.

Some feminists refer to the Spirit as she, thus at the least recalling the feminine gender of the Hebrew word *ruah,* perhaps also identifying some divine characteristic that we associate with the Spirit as female. I find it problematic to reintroduce into American English archaic gender distinctions, and I judge it a no-win situation were the Trinity to be constituted by two he's and one she. So just as I do not refer to God as he, I am not one to call the Spirit she.

When I say that the Spirit gives God the depth feminists need, I mean more than a feminized Spirit. I mean that both the traditional hierarchical God and the church's focus on Jesus Christ can, and often have, become static. Religion can freeze: a throne up there, a cross over here. Such-and-such are sacred, other things profane: the distinctions familiar to religion creep over the body like *rigor mortis,* and we doubt that, lingering in the extremities, life is ready to leap up. I wonder whether some feminists who have left the church have done so for just this reason: with little or no Spirit around, the church looks two dimensional, flattened, no curves, no surprises, no hope for a vigorous breath. Encased by the wood of the pews we all get prematurely interred, like poor Thomas à Kempis, who when his body was exhumed was discovered to have waked up from the coma during which he was mistakenly buried and to have clawed away to open the lid of his coffin. A lively Spirit might give just what we need: like the daughter of Jairus, once lying dead, we can now jump up, dance around the room, and have supper with family and friends.

with requisite rituals . . .

each Sunday morning

Many college students claim that they can be Christian without going to church. This is not merely adolescent irresponsibility: many adults also understand their Christian faith as a personal worldview that does not depend upon or generate any communal ritual behavior. What with the popular idea of "the separation of church and state" and the Enlightenment conviction that religion is merely one's individual value system, people think of religion, rather like one's bathroom habits, as perhaps wholesome but surely not a focus for public celebration. As well, many feminists feel themselves so excluded from the Sunday event that they also, although still affirming the faith, reject the ritual.

I am over fifty years old. My parents brought me to church each week since shortly after my birth. At college a thousand of us students went to the enormous university chapel for worship every Sunday. I estimate that I miss perhaps two weeks per year for sickness and one week per year because of travel schedules. When my daughters were small, I missed some Sundays to care for them when sick. I cannot recall a single Sunday in my life that I simply chose to stay home. This computes to approximately 2400 Sundays that I have attended church. Let me try to explain why I keep it up.

If you grant that, at least in its fullest manifestation, religion is a communal worldview, then we must inquire into religion's rituals, for rituals it will have. Rituals are the communal enactments of a group's myths. The group retells its favorite stories and enacts its beliefs, to remind itself of its values and to announce them to the world. It's commonplace for college students to scorn ritual as restrictive and boring. Yet when I look out over (a) thirty pairs of jeans, (b) fifteen baseball caps and (c) three tatoos, I see in their ritual attire, as plainly as if displayed on a billboard, (a) my students' embrace of the myth of casual equality à la the American frontier, (b) their group bonding over televised war games and (c) a bit of stereotypical initiatory scarification. And when the freshmen men arrive at class with diapers over their jeans, we all know that fraternity pledge week has pulled them down into the depths of brotherhood. So, to some rituals no, to others yes.

For ritual to accomplish its task well, two conditions will need to be met: the myth must be believed, and the enactment must be dynamic. Most college students accept the myth of absolute equality; they believe that simple dress improves their state of mind; they judge meticulous attire to be pretense; there is something of the cowboy in each of them. Many know their jeans, brand by brand, and wear this ritual dress with intent. When I wear my jeans to match a blue African necklace, everyone knows it doesn't count. They believe the myth, I don't.

Lately we've all heard about clitoridectomies. News reports give graphic descriptions of the gruesome ritual, but in all the recent publicity I have not seen reference to the myth the ritual enacts, a myth that at least some of its adherents believe. According to some traditional African cosmogonies, humans were created and are born as bisexual beings. This formation is a primordial mistake which the community must correct. The female soul must be excised from the man, the male soul from the female. To render both genders fit for useful life, part of each must be cut off. I study this myth with chagrin: we will not be able to stop clitoridectomies with some one-hour video presentation about a female's health and well-being. At least some people enact this ritual because they believe it: not merely its patriarchal by-products, but also its religious components.

The goal of ritual is communal strengthening. Alas for an increasingly privatized society, ritual has only secondarily to do with individual feelings. In fact, the ritual is a substitute for personal choice, almost an antidote to individual preference. The value of me concedes to the value of us, at least for the duration of the ritual. Ideally, my personal preference supports the group values; I have chosen the group identity. Yet in the ritual, the focus is not on my feelings but on group process. To enter wholeheartedly into the ritual, one must move from private choice to communal engagement, beyond the boundaries of me into the sea of the others. This transition is extremely difficult for a person of my introverted, introspective personality.

Sometimes the ritual fools you. A bride may think that her unique self is the center of the wedding. Actually, the event, perhaps more than any other in her life, except for graduations, inserts her into a largely predetermined role, and although she picks which version of the uniform to wear, she is more that day a bride than she is herself. Entire books compete to choreograph her every move. There is ritual wisdom in this: a wedding is not a display of the two individuals' love for each other. A wedding is a communal enactment of a social reorganization. From now on everyone, even the Internal Revenue Service, will view these two as belonging together, and that alteration in the communal order is what the wedding ritual is about.

Now to Sunday morning.

I am all too aware that Christian ritual can be stultifying. Of my 2400 Sunday mornings, few are luminous memories of enacted Easter. As a theologian who is skilled in diagnosing sick ritual, I judge few liturgies wholly healthy. My bet is that I see diseases even where you don't, infections here and there. But I discover that I can't recall many miserable liturgies. My mind throws them out. I don't keep junk around, I am a perpetual emptier of wastebaskets. So I can't regale you with tales of terrible Sundays, incompetent musicians, ignorant clergy, heretical sermons, inarticulate readers, untrained assistants, shallow prayers, silly hymns, thoughtless design, mistaken gestures, flat symbols, plastic flowers, grungy vestments, inattentive action, fake bread, plain bad judgment. Here's the sad truth: what some folk cook up as a great idea isn't. The new stew is not necessarily better than the old one; yet the old one may be tasteless by now, even nauseating.

In some churches the liturgy is particularly cruel for women. I am amazed at how many women remain in churches were they are not allowed to preside or preach, where God is unremittingly termed Father and King and He, where texts call the human community "man," where Eve is blamed for sin. I wish the women in these churches well: I would be out of there, for I would not tolerate the cognitive dissonance between the myth I accept and the myth those rituals enact. As you might guess, I choose carefully which church I attend, at least for the last 1300 Sundays.

Once I got stuck in a Byzantine Catholic eucharist. Although the assembly was filled with Western Ph.D.s and the presider was a perfectly normal and likeable man from Baltimore, you'd think we had beamed back into another millennium, traveled through a holy stargate into an alien culture. I watched the ceremony from the balcony and did not participate as the priest inserted a holy spoon with its mixture of bread crumbs and wine into each communicant's mouth. I could not recognize in this archaic hierarchical ritual the trinitarian faith of an American feminist Christian. I do not contest that in another world this liturgy may have served well. But it was not the ritual of the I-who-I-are.

But usually I am not in the balcony glowering. Usually I am near the front, more or less engaged, hoping that by means of the ritual I will experience the following four things: marking the myth; living beyond choice; praising God; and finding myself inserted in community.

I use only the old-fashioned calendars on which Sunday is the first day of the week. Especially for desk calendars—reports my daughter after her annual efforts at Christmas shopping—these are getting more and more difficult to find. But as Christian tradition says, it was on the first day of the week that God created light, that Christ rose from the dead, and that the Spirit came into the community. I choose to recall these myths by marking the day. I don't keep Sunday as a Calvinist sabbath, with no work, no play. But I experience the day as a new beginning. My pace is slower. We use a tablecloth at dinner. I avoid unpleasant chores. Life need not be one damn day after another, and keeping Sunday is a sign of the distinction between days, of the hope that resurrection surprises tedium and death.

Fifty years of habit and conviction mean that I do not decide each Sunday whether to go to church. Were I sick, I could choose against it, but I do not have to decide for it week by week: the commitment has already been made. In a socio-economic class in which options are perpetually, exponentially, opening before me, every meal a choice in the midst of abundance, each activity a decision among dozens of possibilities, Sunday morning presents me with a time beyond choice. I have read that one psychological outcome of the information explosion is increasing indecision. You can't make up your mind or commit to anything because, well, in two minutes there might be a better option appearing on the screen. However, some things in life are presented to me: my genes, my family, my death, my children's life decisions. Over these I have little or no control. The discipline of attending church each week gives me practice in life beyond choice.

I was taught that the primary purpose of Sunday worship was just that: the worship of God. If there is a God, that God is to be honored. As a person who still fiercely advocates thank-you notes, I judge an attitude of gratefulness a good thing, not only religiously appropriate, but also psychologically healthy and socially desirable. Cynics are depressing, complainers a bore.

But why not honor God with a morning walk through the park? I now argue that the primary effect of Sunday worship is insertion into community. At least in my socio-economic class, persons are increasingly alone, eating at the microwave, commuting by oneself, watching one's favorite program alone on one of the household TVs. I hear that bowling as a hobby continues strong, but that membership in bowling clubs is down. However, religion is not about bowling alone. A trinitarian faith implies that you can't get God by yourself, and the Trinity isn't a divine monad. Whether you want it or not, God's Spirit brings along with it the rest of the world: the circle of believers, the saints glorious and disgusting, "everyone according to their needs" in the intercessions. I am not always glad to be thrown in with all those others—that pastor, those parishioners, the sick and the poor whom we pray for. Probably if I made up my own religion, I'd invent an easier one, with less commitment to others and more walks in the park. The Sunday ritual reinserts me regularly into the often troublesome commitment to God in the others.

Being at church connects my whole week to that of other Christians. Is it Lent? We'll eat more simply. Are we in the fifty days of Easter? Then even a Tuesday is somehow like the resurrection. Perhaps it's the mustard-seed-becoming-the-tree-of-life week, or it's Mary-singing-the-Magnificat-to-Elizabeth week. I think about the season or the readings, like a manifestation of Jung's collective unconscious, being in Christians all around the world.

As for my feminism: The liturgies I normally attend insert me into a church formed by a tradition of androcentrism, yet being reshaped by women's perceptions and with women's leadership at all levels. Old hymns call God king, and new hymns praise God as mother, wisdom, tree of life. The biblical readings tell of more men than women, but in sermons neither of my male pastors refers to God as he. The eucharistic prayer that my pastor is using, the one in our church's new worship book that praises God as Guide and Rock and Water—well, I was on the team that wrote the prayer. The community, although rooted in patriarchy, is growing steadily toward feminism, in some ways behind and in other ways ahead of the secular world. So I sense little cognitive dissonance between my Sunday mornings and my Wednesday afternoons. Instances of blight or blossom are similar.

So I mark the mythic first day of the week by a pattern of commitment in which, as I praise God, I find myself inserted in the human community, which, I discover again and again, is full of needy people. And my religious tradition says that the way I am to attend to God is to attend to them. It's understandable that I may not want to go to church. Like the woman in Wallace Stevens' poem "Sunday Morning," I could stay home, wearing a peignoir and contemplating the divine within the self. But to be honest, I can't. All I'd think all morning is, why aren't I at church? And then I'd check the appointed readings, to bring the liturgy to me, even though I had not brought myself to it.

Like everyone else, I wish that the church's community would be a remarkable sign of divine transformation. I wish the liturgy was feminist heaven, the adult forums vibrant discussions of profound religious issues, the parish activities stunning aftershocks of the resurrection. Perhaps it is not the perception of what Sunday morning is that keeps people away: it is the heartache over what it isn't. Indeed, some Sundays I experience such a wrench, desperate disappointment, sorrow to the marrow. But again I think, ah yes, the trinitarian faith: if this God became incarnate in a first-century male and lives continuously in the human community, I ought not expect Sunday morning to be an hour in the garden of Eden. If your God is incarnate, the garden might be like more Gethsemani. The Christian enterprise is not getting yourself transported to heaven. Rather, it is realizing that this unkempt community is the paradise that the Spirit of God is cultivating. I do not always succeed in this realization, but each Sunday morning I try.

in the night of Easter

Despite the cultural and commercial popularity of Christmas, it is Easter that determines the Christian faith. And before I describe why and how I ritualize the resurrection, I wish to distance myself from two more familiar observances of Easter.

The first is the Easter Day Extravaganza. Vast numbers of people return to church for their annual glance at religion, and by their passive stupefaction during the service they indicate their unfamiliarity with any movement the community has made throughout the last fifty-one weeks. The service lasts twice as long as usual, what with robed choirs parading around and half the annual music budget spent on hired instrumentalists. The flower bill alone could feed a family for some time.

I find this springtime ceremony inadequate for the deepest tasks of religion. It is little more than a flower festival, and I ask how the sun shining on the flowers blooming in the northern hemisphere in April can be a sufficient response to the evils in human life.

A second way to ritualize Easter is a hold-over from the medieval contemplation on death. Now, it's important to acknowledge that religion will always attend to death. Religion is the system of symbols and rituals which addresses humankind's ultimate problems, and it is evident that our fears and sorrows when facing death are paramount among these problems. But sometimes, for example during Europe's late Middle Ages, religion's requisite concern with death becomes its primary obsession. Perhaps in those precarious centuries, the only surety in a limited life was death, and thus death overwhelmed both one's life and religion's rituals. I think of the sarcophagus in a Finnish church, constructed like a bunkbed: the statuary on the upper level depicts the aristocratic couple in fine attire, and the lower level shows their skeletons, replete with engorged snakes and rats in the ribcages. Lay out, side by side, graphic crucifixes and stations of the cross and a literal hell and a rigorous penance practice and martyrs' bones and the conviction that God punishes personal sins by meting out particularly unpleasant deaths, and you have a belief system confronting death at every turn.

In many places and times, the observance of Holy Week transferred this focus on death to Christ. The days were spent in somber contemplation of Calvary. In some contemporary Central American communities, the elaborate pageantry that engages the entire town concludes, not on Easter, but on Good Friday. It's all about death: the ritual requires the people to look death in the face, and they do it, magnificently, heroically, and then it's over. The theory of atonement most popular with catechists of past centuries complemented all this death. That our sins merited our death and that Christ substituted his death for ours gave theological support to the stranglehold that death had on society.

As a feminist, I reject also this cemetery parade. Along with many other Christians, I do not subscribe to the beliefs that God sends death to punish personal failings and, as old hymns suggest, that the sufferings of Jesus were the worst in human history. I ask how one man's death can be the solution to the continuing deaths of the weak. All this death gets us nowhere.

That Jesus died was not, for the first several centuries of the church, the central point. Everyone dies, one way or another. It was rather "the resurrection" that constituted the church. In my piety, Jesus' death has significance both because it proves God's life as a human and it demonstrates the horrific might of injustice; but Jesus' death has its power for me because of the resurrection. Good Friday I observe, waiting, not for a trumpet parade on Easter morning, but for the Easter vigil, a lengthy resurrection celebration that goes on in the middle of Saturday night and is the most feminist liturgical event of the Christian ritual year.

But you ask, what do I mean by "the resurrection," Jesus' resurrection, our own? I have before me John Updike's poem "Seven Stanzas at Easter."[16] It is a stern, even panicked, demand for realism: "if the cells' dissolution did not reverse, the molecules reknit, the amino acids rekindle,/ the Church will fall." Even the angel at the tomb must be, Updike writes, "a real angel ... vivid with hair." "Let us not mock God with metaphor," he writes—an odd demand, it has seemed to me since college days, from a man whose trade is metaphor.

I do not know what Updike meant by the "real" hair of an angel. The tradition of theologians would not agree with Updike: whatever we mean by "angels" does not necessitate their having hair. Indeed, in religion we often see what is not there. A vision of the power of God need not include, as Updike demands, a robe "in real linen/ spun on a definite loom" in order to be a vehicle of divine mercy.

Likewise Updike's fierce cry for the literalness of a resurrected body would not find consensus in the church, not in the Bible, not through most of church history, and not now. And so, Mr. Updike, despite your Lutheran upbringing, I say to you: I cannot concur with your requirements for the resurrection. (And: do all the crosses in all your novels dangle on a gold chain in a woman's cleavage?) Christians borrowed the language of resurrection from earlier Jewish belief that God would vindicate all the righteous martyrs by establishing them, body intact, in the promised land at the end of time. The language indicates that, quite different from the Greeks, the Jews could not imagine a disembodied human self. The New Testament writers give various explanations of what the resurrection, first realized by Jesus, was like. The risen Christ ate meals, and yet whatever his body was could transmigrate in a way human cells cannot. Paul is at pains to describe the wholly new kind of body that the resurrection points to, precisely not like the old one with its molecules and amino acids.

What the biblical writers did agree on was that after the death of Jesus the community shared a life-altering realization that death had been reversed. Its power was broken. Fear was dissipated. Evil and injustice and sorrow and sickness and misery appear to have all the cards, but amazingly God wins in the end. This is not "the flowers that bloom in the spring, tra-la" of sentimental songs, or Walt Whitman's assertion that "the smallest sprout shows there is really no death."[17] Christians take death and the evil that intensifies its horror with absolute seriousness. They attend to the crucifixion. Yet they can unite to counteract evil, transformed by the spirit that was released in the life of Christ.

I do not know what happened to Jesus' body. The Bible offers one possibility: his body was buried but then stolen by those who reverenced his life. Another possibility is that, with his frightened followers in hiding, his body got dumped on a trash heap along with those of other executed prisoners. Faith trains me to say that Christ "is risen," that he entered a new dimension, a second and perfected reality that awaits us all at the end of time. What I believe is that God brought about a transformation so total as to be almost unbelievable: the body of Christ, no longer in Jesus' rotted flesh and bones, is now in our community, which is to recreate the entire world, to witness as God raises up all the world's people to more abundant life.

I ritualize this faith at the Easter vigil. We meet at ten o'clock at night, outside. Perhaps it's raining. Often it's cold. No Easter bonnets here. Wool sweaters. The darkness reminds us of death: no sun and flowers mute the truth. Usually only a small number of us is present, since the service, restored from the church's earlier centuries, is only now catching on again. Standing around, we watch as the new fire is struck, hoping the presider's vestments won't ignite—I remember the year that the clay pot exploded and the kindling flew towards our faces—and we spread the light around with candles, each sharing in the circle of illumination, each making the circle brighter. We are a dark cave welcoming in the light, embracing it, as a waiting womb might admit its future. Then we walk together inside for an hour of readings and songs, many voices from the past, each one read by a different voice in our community—have you heard an eight-year-old read the Sacrifice of Isaac?—and a woman leads us in Miriam's dance at the Red Sea, and all the stories and songs are versions of the one story: that God is creating all things new. We read not the infamous Genesis 3 story about sin and shame and death, but the majestic poem in Genesis 1 about women and men equal in God's image and everything being very good. And then we baptize, pouring buckets of water over infants or adults, and we all get ourselves wet again, remembering birth, being reborn. And finally, sometime after midnight, we move into the pews for the gospel, always the narrative of the women who first told the story that Jesus was raised from death. Then come the bells and the lights and the flowers and the organ and the hymns full of Alleluias and the meal of bread and wine, the body of Christ not in a tomb near Jerusalem but in the freshly baked loaf of bread shared by the community. We are glad for a bite to eat in the middle of the night. The bread and wine will keep us upright until we get home and begin the chocolate feast.

(What?! Your church doesn't do this?)

C. G. Jung lamented that this vigil, which he described as a feminine ritual, was no longer practiced. But it is being restored in churches throughout the world, all roundness and dark and candles and voices and chanting and dancing and bathing and eating, all of us infants again, all of us crones with grand sagas to narrate, all of us the women at the tomb. The vigil is the opposite of a Gothic cathedral, with its solid stone and rigid columns and men marching around telling other people what to do. Vibrant, flowing, the vigil ritualizes the belief that God is the womb within which the community comes to life.

The next morning, after several hours of sleep, I go back to church again, more for old time's sake than for the faith—which are, please understand, two wholly different motivations for attending worship. All the flowered dresses and the sun grinning through the colored windows seem naive, insufficient for the tasks of religion—anyone can sing in broad daylight—whereas last night's dark circle proclaimed in astonishing honesty our acknowledgement of death and our faith in life from God.

and in the dead of winter

C hristians are supposed to know that their preeminent ritual is Easter. But American capitalism prefers Christmas as the ritual of new life, strings of blinking lights having shortcircuited our brains, all those expensive presents purchased in the short days of December a Republican's idea of resurrection for sure. Retail clerks tell of frenzied customers screaming at them when their maxed-out credit cards get rejected, the promise of their monthly bill greater than the grace of the lending institutions. I try to have all my shopping done before Thanksgiving, hoping to avoid altogether pop singers blasting out Christmas carols over the malls' sound systems. Yes, I agree: giving presents is one of the many partial ways—I think of coloring eggs at Easter—that we ritualize God's gift of life. But No to uncontrolled December looting.

Neither is Christmas midnight mass my preferred way to ritualize feminist Christian faith. At midnight mass, I am too tired to tolerate with any grace all the noisy hype—the paid instrumentalists and giggling teenagers and uncontrolled kids in fake velvet and sighing grandparents in red plaid, all the "virgin undefiled" and "silent night" of it all.

Most of what disgusts this feminist is, however, not the Bible's fault. Neither the apostle Paul, nor Mark, the earliest gospel, nor John, the New Testament's symbolic jewel, narrates a birth story. And even in Matthew and Luke, the tale of the virgin birth is not about Mary's anatomy or sex life. A gentle No to "undefiled" language. The virginal conception—to use accurate terminology—is about Jesus coming wholly from God, rather than from the male sperm which pre-scientific authors considered the quintessential source of human life. To articulate the belief that Jesus came from God, the evangelists borrowed cultural imagery from Greco-Roman myths, in which numerous superbeings were miraculously generated. And a No to Silent Night. If a woman named Mary was in labor, the night wasn't silent, despite the fantasies of later celibates who claimed that asexuality is perfection, that Mary conceived through her ear, and that Jesus' birth, as miraculous as the conception, had occurred without tearing Mary's hymen or giving her any pain.

Christmas Day is different. Few people come. A gentle calm holds us in a space emptied of enthusiasm. The Isaiah reading promises that we will witness God's mighty arm. I think quietly (all the trumpeters are home opening presents) of an infant's prehensile grip, and of my friend's retarded son born without this primitive hold on life. I picture, side by side, the tiny arm of the newborn in the manger and God's outstretched arm holding back the Red Sea and leading the Israelites to safety. Yes to Psalm 98 with the rivers clapping their hands. Yes to the serious Christmas carol "What child is this," with the nails piercing his hands in the second stanza. Yet on Christmas Day, although we see the creche set up near the altar, we follow Paul, Mark, and John: we do not read the highly questionable Bethlehem tale. Rather, we read the poem from John 1, which is not about a baby boy, but rather about the solstice.

As a child attending a conservative parochial school at which scientific learning and attunement with nature were low priority items, I did not even know the word "solstice." Now, thanks to ecological awareness and the revival of neo-paganism, solstice is everywhere. Stationery companies make money selling solstice cards. Churches host solstice concerts featuring whale songs. For some people, the day functions as the primary pantheist festival, valuable both as a celebration of nature and an antidote to Christmas. Predating ceremonies for patriarchal boy-kings, solstice celebrates the primordial womb, the mother night of the year knowing its own darkness, the female power of the cave nurturing its hibernating self. For wiccans at solstice, day yields to night, the God in heaven to the goddess of earth, a supernatural deity to the powerful self, and they delight around the symbol of the evergreen.

I have never been sentimental about nature. Friedrich Schleiermacher's exaltation of women as closer than men to pristine nature strikes me as Aristotelian sexism cooking up the old stew in a new pot. Henry David Thoreau relied on tools from Ralph Waldo Emerson and food from Louisa May Alcott's family to survive there at Walden Pond, just as privileged Western women don silk underwear for their midnight ritual in the park and campers purchase a high-tech water filter to enjoy the wild. I have read the diaries of the pioneer women who walked across the American prairie, eating their oxen and burying their children along the way. Rachel Calof recorded her years homesteading in North Dakota: blizzards, hailstorms, starvation, disease, accidents, lack of fuel, a five mile walk for water, and horrendous childbirths. And I say: at least be honest about Mother Nature, who serves up death as well as life. In hyena litters, the dominant newborn's first task is to murder its siblings so that only one suckling commands its mother's milk.

Solstice speaks of the balance of death and life. The thought of residing in a climate warm all year around startles me by its deception: I want to see the tree skeletons in December, to wrap myself in goose down and so withstand the cold. We keep solstice in our home, for a reason that partakes of death: since my divorce, my daughters spend Christmas with their father, and so my husband and I celebrate solstice with them. We do not pretend it is Christmas. End-of-Advent time, we sing in harmony all the Advent hymns that beg God for light. But since this feasting and lighting-the-candles and thanking-the-evergreen were occasioned by the death of my first marriage, the celebration is an honest balance, some light on the dark day, a plea that God will bring us through the death we are all so good at, so used to. "O Dayspring, splendor of light everlasting, come and enlighten those who sit in darkness and in the shadow of death," we pray as our solstice prayer, the medieval monastics providing the words for our contemporary blended family.

Thus, for me, solstice is about the cycle of death and life in the universe, in family systems, in me. The trees outside look like Victorian hatracks, all empty wood, and inside the house is an enormous evergreen: we smile at this reverse of normalcy. But a dance around an evergreen is not enough. It is something, but not enough. My youthful attempt at everlasting love died. This evergreen will die, its needles already falling into our baseboard radiator. But I am not a hyena, killing my siblings for life. I am a human nursed on meaning. I hope that the pinpoint of light in the cave is not only the beginning of spring but also a symbol of transformative ecstasy.

So I move from December 21 to the 25th, from solstice songs to John's poem. The first three centuries of Christians didn't observe Jesus' birth in any way, but finally, at the Christianizing of the Roman Empire, the solstice was selected as the appropriate time to celebrate the incarnation. And those of us who make it to church on Christmas morning encounter this solstice in the sublime gospel reading of John 1. Here is no charming fairy-tale version of a birth: rather, "The life was the light of all people. The light shines in the darkness, and the darkness did not overcome it." Shivering in the cold of the northern hemisphere, we await God's light.

Theologians call this embodiment of divine light the incarnation. The God of monotheists is a transcendent being, not only located in my mind but actually existing beyond time, outside space, without gender, not merely superhuman but transcending all we humans know or imagine. But the God of Christians is more than transcendent. This God chooses, here and there, now and then, to enter human time and space. This is not pantheism: as a Christian I cannot claim that the trees are god or that I am goddess. Rather, the deity, who is outside our world in some mystery, not only can inhabit also this world, but did once take on a specific human body. At Christmas, Christians celebrate the hope that God can come to be where God was not. I often wonder if this is true, the God part, the incarnation part: as a Christian I try to believe it.

Christians borrow from solstice the natural metaphor of a reversal of the status quo, of hope beyond experience. Light shines in the darkness, the divine transforms the human. Yet while adopting the solstice metaphor, the writer of John 1 goes further. God is more than spring swallowing winter, more than a second marriage following a divorce. I recall that in the first creation story in Genesis, God's light shone for three days before God made the sun: grace encompasses nature, yet grace is more than nature. Christian faith claims that the natural cycle genuflects toward God, whose light is finally everlasting, whose life ultimately eternal. Christians say that God's light in the person Jesus is more brilliant than the sun at the turn of the earth's orbit in the dead of winter, God's life in the Spirit more vital than a universe that eons ago had its beginning and will some day have its end. And so I say: I too am more than a body. My task on earth is not merely to reproduce the species. The natural cycles of even me is not all there is. Before me is the promise of yet another year in which to embody life beyond life.

Then we go home and open presents.

we savor the water, the bread, the wine

L et me describe to you how the sacraments were celebrated (to use a rather inappropriate verb) in the church of my childhood. First baptism.

Typically, uncomfortable in those lace ruffles and cap, and having absorbed the tension from its mother's arms, the infant brought to baptism was cranky. The parents, godparents, and baby arrived at the Sunday service after the sermon, just in time for the rite of baptism to begin. Inside the bowl of the font was a glass dish in which was half a cup of water. The pastor read a page about sin, and the adults mumbled the baby's name once and "yes" several times, and then, very carefully, so as not to get anything too wet, the pastor dripped water three times on the baby's forehead. The child thus having been saved from hell, the whole group trooped out of the church. At our family's baptisms, our entourage created quite a stir by attending the entire service.

As for eucharist: four times a year, on Sunday evenings, the faithful returned to church for a second time that day for a service of Holy Communion. The mood was penitential, the hymns lugubrious. The ushers lined us up at the communion rail, where we knelt to receive a thin white wafer and a sip of wine. Back at our pews we knelt again, demonstrating our sorrow for the sin which had occasioned the death of Christ that this ritual recalled. Not a single child attended, for one had to be past puberty to participate. From the balcony came somber background music. When my brother learned to play the organ, he spelled the organist who could then commune: my brother would put his fingers on the downpressed keys so that as the organist got off the bench, there would be no break in the chords that surrounded the room like violet Victorian drapes.

The earnest if not grim enactment of these rituals meant to point us to the death of Christ and our participation in it. I am told that still today in the hinterlands of Norway, some Lutherans commune twice in their life, at puberty and on their deathbed, all that focus on sin and forgiveness being too much to endure more often. One clergyman described in a lecture how he'd hold the infant high and yell out, "Today we are celebrating the death of this baby!" It is as if, no different from the Aztec sun god, our deity requires death as payment for life. We'd give God Christ's death, and the symbolic death of the baby, and the death of our sins, and just like with 1950s green stamps, the redemption center would give us back a coffee pot. The question is, of course, to what extent we actually did receive back a life alive enough to embody, to share, to savor.

Perhaps you can see why, when young women tell me of their despair over the church, I exclaim my astonishment at how much the church has changed in fifty years. For now we see mainstream Protestant and Roman Catholic churches with large baptismal pools, baptisms that involve the entire parish, weekly communion in the morning's light, the pastor crouching down to meet the height of the three-year-olds who are receiving a hunk of real bread. One could argue that most of the reforms advocated by the ecumenical liturgical movement—lively use of natural symbols, circular rather than rectangular space, participatory ritual rather than passive attention to clerical leadership, a text reflective of our place and time, the multiplicity of voices in the assembly—express the same spirit that the feminist movement describes. That the baptism ritual will actually recall birth, its plentiful messy waters, its laughter and its cries, is a win for feminism. That the eucharist will actually resemble a meal, with good-tasting freshly-baked bread, the sparkle of wine, and the participants alert and looking at one another around the table, signifies that God's grace is no longer construed as a passing grade handed over to a nearly failing student by a dour professor, who knows you deserve to flunk, but instead gives you a C for Christ's sake.

I do not mean to advocate Joy Land, the sacraments celebrated with giddy grins. I recall those 1960s *agape* meals with red balloons on the tables and everyone's mood as high as helium. These events were fun, but I know today, with my sister-in-law dying of cancer, that they were immature: as with crying, laughing is not enough. That baby we goo over, perhaps the parents are distraught over the birth, quarreling over a secret sorrow we haven't guessed. Our Sophia dances must somehow include also the woman watching from her wheelchair.

This is what I advocate: water, bread, and wine, representing all the water before my birth and around the globe, all the bread that nourishes our bodies, all the wine that bonds our community; this water, bread, and wine, savored as the pith of life; with these three quintessential symbols the community praising God, who is Water and Bread and Wine beyond our experience, Life and Death beyond our imaginings. The sacraments call us into our most intense awareness of our genuine self, of the other, and of God. And despite a twentieth century of improvement, we've got a long way to go.

In John's gospel, on the evening of Maundy Thursday, Jesus doesn't eat the joyous passover meal with his disciples. Rather, to show the sacrament of the body of Christ, Jesus washes their feet. Through this primordial human use of water— we wash the newborn, we wash our hands, we wash the dying and the dead—the church has seen that Christ's body is no longer only the flesh of a person named Jesus, and not only in sanctified bread. The body of our God is now manifest in the feet of the community, toenail fungus and bunions notwithstanding, and we honor that God by kneeling, not before some glorious image of God, but before one another, towel in hand.

Obsession with my sin can be mere solipsism, adoration of the crucified can be only morbidity. The sacraments employ the most fundamental necessities of human life—water, staple food, and festal drink—because it is this community and the health of its body that the mercy of God pursues. The sacraments mean to bring us into the life and death of God realized in one another and to train us in savoring such odd divinity.

following saints unbalanced

As a child I knew nothing about Catherine of Siena. The Lutheranism in which I was reared avoided the saints like the plague, as if one could catch the deadly disease of Roman Catholicism by being exposed to them, as if the saints were like the rats carrying the fleas of Works Righteousness. We knew you didn't have to be exemplary to be saved—a comforting idea for all those unremarkable German peasant farmers—and we didn't waste much time venerating people who might have been. We called the biblical Paul a saint, but virtually no one else, not Mary, not even Martin Luther. The word was reserved for what all baptized people would be in heaven.

As a woman I was introduced to the saints through snippets of their writings. Quoted in liturgical histories and cited in epigraphs, the voluminous works of the saints were edited down into tantalizing sound bites. Their foreign worldview was cut out, their craziness was cooked away; what was served up was a palatable contemporary Christian stew flavored with spices from the past. Julian called God her clothing; Pseudo-Dionysius wrote that God is "not greatness, not smallness, not living, not life, not king, not wisdom, not sonhood, not fatherhood"[18]; Meister Eckhart spoke of nonGod: I drank these quotations down, I consumed them, starved for words with more flavor than those in our catechism. I realized that the language I used in worship had been treasured by these writers, that the brilliance of their words illumined my way as a Christian thinker. I was into saint veneration.

But then—the loss of another innocence!—I studied more. I read entire sermons, complete essays, whole works, biographies of their lives. And now it seemed as if the saints were aliens from another solar system, creatures with far different brains and inexplicable values. How could I venerate these bizarre characters? Did intense religious devotion always bring on this craziness? I wondered whether facility and creativity in religious language necessarily transported the speaker far far away from the world I wanted to inhabit.

For example, back to Catherine of Siena.

When first learning about her, I honored Catherine for being a more stunning Perpetua. Like the third-century martyr, fourteenth-century Catherine was a woman who knew her own mind and fearlessly acted upon her own convictions. She rejected her proper role in society, stood up against authority figures, grounded her self-awareness in her religious faith, and recorded her visions of God so that others could attest that the divine had visited her. A Protestant, I did not respond well to Catherine's head in a glass case on an altar in Siena, but as a woman writing in the church I revered her "O fiery abyss of charity! O eternal beauty, O eternal wisdom, O eternal goodness, O eternal mercy! O immeasurable generosity!"[19] She said that Christ calls us "trees of love," and in public lectures I repeat her image of the Trinity as Table, Food, and Waiter. She tutored me in the language of ecstacy that Lutheran parochial schools had never, ever, admitted.

However, knowing that Catherine had stopped eating at age thirty-three led me to read Caroline Walker Bynum's analysis of such women. Bynum's deeply disturbing data and one hundred and twenty pages of endnotes about the lives of dozens of women who like Catherine were obsessed with food and fasting led me to emulate the scholar Bynum more than the unbalanced women she described. I am struck by the enormity of the great gulf fixed between these women and ourselves. Of course, we doubt the veracity of accounts of women subsisting for years without consuming any food whatsoever. But I stand mute before a spirituality that revered even the appearance of such behavior. Apparently we have here not typical adolescent anorexia nervosa, but rather an exceedingly complex interplay of female identification with food, lay celibate women's religious imagination, medieval eucharistic piety, and a spirituality that lusted after suffering—none of which I share. And so Catherine, along with many other women whose writings I had admired, refused food, regularly vomited up minuscule meals, drank the pus of the sick, and experienced ecstacy by, as they said, being nursed on the milk of the eucharistic host.

I find all this alien, even repellent, not the least because I need food, a lot of it, preferably three times a day. If dinner is served at eight rather than six, I begin to lose clarity, and personality deterioration sets in. I smile at Teresa of Avila's advice: when rather too many Carmelite nuns were experiencing visions, Teresa ordered the sisters to eat more food. In Lent, I eat more simply, and on Good Friday eat my grandmother's purgative ritual meal of noodles and prunes, but I do not fast. Although some Christians claim that fasting brings them closer to

God, I judge fasting a Platonic denial of the good body God made, one of those precarious religious exercises that courts life by flirting with death. Fasting reduces me to a furtive animal, eyes jerking back and forth looking for food. I think of Phillip Melanchthon, premier lay theologian of the Reformation, lying near death of physical and emotional collapse, and Martin Luther ordering him to eat on pain of excommunication. Melanchthon ate, and lived. So as I plan out next week's menus, I wonder: what shall I think of Catherine?

Some people think that the Bible is a lengthy narrative about exemplary people. Ha!—hardly a one. Even the court history of King David includes the minority reports, one noble tale followed by an ignoble one, the religious community already back then disagreeing about whose behavior served as a model for faithful living. Yes, women dedicated themselves to lives of prayer, but they renounced their parents to do so. What did I expect from human beings, especially ones trying to live beyond their culture? As my daughter's T-shirt says, "Give me ambiguity or give me something else." Catherine was shaped by her culture, she no less than I, her hunger to consume Christ no more than mine to write a religious bestseller. The trick is how to wring meaning out of our cultural preoccupations, making them more, making them less, making them other, so that within our culture we serve more than our culture's values and our own culturally-formed egos, but one another and perhaps even God.

I call Catherine a Christian proto-feminist. Despite her repeated reference to herself as a "miserable creature" and her body a "stinking garment," which strikes our therapeutic generation as a neurotically negative view of the laywoman, she lived out her life's choices with a fierce integrity that stuns us even today. She pulled others along her path, throwing people—family, friends, followers, politicians, bishops, the pope—off balance, challenging them to see somehow beyond their normal sights. She exemplifies what recent scholarship has demonstrated, that it is historically inaccurate to claim that Christianity always oppressed women. Far from beating all women down, the Christian faith became, for at least some women, the rocket they rode into the skies. Their faith licensed them to begin creating the feminism I enjoy. All those celibate medieval women achieving amenorrhea by diet, trying in the only way they knew to control and limit their menstrual flow: I see that they were not so pathological as I first thought.

So Catherine, teetering on her no-food tightrope, falling off at thirty-three— if that was a good age for Jesus to die, it'd work fine for her—is, in an ironic way, a woman to follow. Not "to follow" as in "to mimic." Copying her borderline behavior these days would get me institutionalized. No: rather, "to follow" as in "to follow after," to teeter along in my time, as she did in hers, hoping to live through my culture into a deeper life. I cannot be sentimental about Catherine, or indeed about any of the unbalanced saints whose lives both fascinate and disgust us. Indeed, in confronting Catherine, the feminist Christian encounters a proto-type of the church: it is not what we wish it were; even when it inspires, it also troubles, and sometimes it repels. Catherine would not, could not, live now, and it would be anachronistic, perhaps sick, perhaps even immoral, to model our lives on hers. But, by introducing into my life just a tad of the classic ritual of saint vener-ation, I can carry something of her spirit like a baby alive inside me; I hope that in bearing the Christian tradition, I discover that God is always being born anew.

attending to their remains

One saint who was not crazy was Radegund. Born a pagan Germanic princess in about 520 C.E., the child Radegund was kidnapped in battle by the Christian Frankish king Chlotar and was reared in a convent to become one of his simultaneous wives. By the time she came of age, however, she was a devout Christian who preferred the life of prayer to the violence of the court, and after a short noncompliant married life she left the king and established a convent that became one of France's centers of learning. At first the local bishop, fearful of reprisal from the king, refused to cooperate with the queen's request, but the story goes that Radegund veiled herself and set up the convent anyway. I first learned about her when studying the unparalleled Latin hymnwriter Venantius Fortunatus: for it was as Radegund's secretary in her Poitiers convent that, at her request to celebrate the convent's having received "a fragment of the True Cross," he composed the two classic hymns that laud the cross as the tree of life, "Vexilla regis" and "Pange lingua gloriosi." We still sing these hymns each Lent. Fortunatus also wrote a biography of Radegund in which he lauds her for all the usual things—eating little, feeding the poor, washing the lepers, healing the sick, even stilling tempests. He mentions nothing of her love of learning, the library she assembled, or her support of his creative writing, noting only his gratitude that this woman, one of the sex "who appeared to be imbeciles,"[20] was crowned with merits by Christ.

And so I visited Poitiers. Poitiers was home also to the eminent bishop and theologian Hilary, but it is Radegund who has won the popularity contest. The church's interior is nearly totally covered with small white marble wall plaques engraved with "Merci" and "Reconnaissance" to Radegund for prayers heard and miracles granted. Her sarcophagus is in the church's crypt, and a woman my age was kneeling beside it in prayer: yet another woman walking across the town or across the continent to be near holy places and precious bones.

I think of Helena, Emperor Constantine's mother, who at age seventy traveled to Jerusalem, climbing up what she claimed were the stairs of Pilate's palace and digging up from the soil of Golgotha what she was convinced was the true

110

cross. I think of Egeria some decades later, traveling from Spain to Jerusalem, visiting biblical sites along the way, meeting with eminent bishops, describing in her travelogue the emotionally charged Holy Week services at the sites Helena had claimed as sacred. I think of amazing Margery Kempe, the fourteenth-century English woman who, after bearing fourteen children, used her inheritance to pay off her husband's debts and in this way negotiated release from his bed, after which she went off on one pilgrimage after another, causing glorious commotion wherever she went, experiencing hysterics when she consumed the body of Christ, grieving aplenty at the sites of Christ's passion and death. "And when they came up on to the Mount of Calvary, she fell down because she could not stand or kneel, but writhed and wrestled with her body, spreading her arms out wide, and cried with a loud voice as though her heart would have burst apart, for in the city of her soul she saw truly and freshly how our Lord was crucified."[21] Are there three male pilgrims as renowned as these three females?

I do not know if, like Helena and Egeria and Margery, I am a pilgrim. Probably not. They journeyed to get closer to God, as if in the paths where Jesus walked or in bones of the saints there was left a residue of holiness, and if one got near enough to the *axis mundi,* one could absorb grace from the aura of divinity. Unlike these three, I am not anxious to travel to the Holy Land, dreading not so much the suicide bombers as the glitched-up, glunked-up taste of past pilgrims who layered their piety onto the pathways and tombs. I smile at Luther's ridicule of the medieval relic trade: as one of his Christmas sermons has it, "And now think what Mary could use for swaddling clothes—some garment she could spare, perhaps her veil—certainly not Joseph's breeches which are now on exhibition at Aachen."[22] But I do visit places marked by the lives of the saints, my travels attending to what remains of their body just as my thoughts attend to what remains of their minds. And I regret that, in accord with his wishes, my father's ashes were scattered at sea. What I wish is that his ashes had been buried, and there, attending to his remains, I could set up a plaque saying "Merci."

Mostly the remains to which I attend are the words, the accounts of their visions, their reflections on their studies. When the attendant of the Library of Congress Rare Book Room brought me a fifteenth-century blockbook *Biblia Pauperum,* I gently touched the pages and, although not wailing like Margery Kempe, I did begin to weep: here it was, here was one of these beloved blockbooks: who had owned it, touched its pages, prayed by its pictures, read its words? I recall seeing Ambrose's skeleton in its glass coffin all dressed up in those unnecessary nineteenth-century brocade vestments, and I thought, ah! all those vibrant metaphors from that small skull! Do you remember Lucy, on her Narnian voyage to Aslan's country, discovering the magician's book? Words can indeed pulse off into the air; the page cannot hold the words down, the words fly free and come to rest here in my very head.

But after reading the words, I go honor the graves. First I read Lucretia Mott's sermons on the equality of women, then I plodded through Philadelphia's cemetery to find her headstone, identical to all the other modest Quaker headstones. I attend first to one set of remains, then to the other. It's another ritual. The gospels report that the women went to the tomb to honor a dead body and there encountered a living reality. So also I travel to tombs, and while my travels may be more tourism than pilgrimage, Poitiers sure beats a cruise to a casino hands down. Although what I honor is bones, my travels are a lifeline from the past down to me.

opening up in prayer

Of the three kinds of Christian prayer—liturgical, contemplative and conversational—I am good at only the first. As a college sophomore, I complained to the campus chaplain about a Sunday's intercessory prayer, then was asked to write the prayer for the following week, and soon afterward found myself hired as a writer for the chapel—which job landed me in my lifelong task of analyzing and crafting the language of prayer. What I wrote then and since were innumerable liturgical intercessions, those communal prayers in the Sunday liturgy that follow a formal outline: "let us pray for the church, let us pray for the world, let us pray for the sick." At their best, such intercessions employ a rhetoric objective enough and a tone centrist enough to gather up the immense diversity of the praying assembly. Liturgical prayer is more or less prescribed, its syntax straightforward, its form and content varying little and slowly over the centuries. Liturgical prayer is not about the me who is, but about the us whom faith hopes we become.

The second kind of prayer, contemplative prayer, became the monastic skill of choice. Although the medieval mystics' talk of abandoning the sick self sounds alien to our ears, I have read with interest every published word of the twentieth-century monk Thomas Merton—as well as many of his unpublished words, since while writing my doctoral dissertation on his poetry, I even tried deciphering his illegible notebooks. So I know how a contemporary person describes contemplative prayer: one tries to go through words, beyond words, into the mystery of God. I can lecture about contemplative prayer, but I do not aspire to it.

The third type of prayer, private daily prayer, is colloquial conversation that assumes God to be an interested and compassionate listener to my human musings. Some believers claim that they chat with God easily, regularly, finding calm and direction in a coffee break with the divine. Conversational prayer imagines an open phone line between me and the omniscient and omnipotent deity. It is not merely my meditation time, an occasion to calm myself down and to sort out priorities. It assumes that the Almighty listens to me, directs my decisions, keeps me from uterine cancer, perhaps arranges the weather to accommodate my plans.

Conversational prayer is connection with God without intermediaries, a theophany without the oracle.

Each year I teach Augustine's *Confessions*. (First: it is tragic, Augustine, that to embody your philosophical and anthropological notions you did not marry your beloved concubine of fifteen years and mother of your son. The difference for one and a half millennia of Christian sex ethics would have been immeasurable.) About a thousand years before any other Westerner, Augustine wrote an autobiography, its role in the development of Western consciousness being, well, immeasurable. The *Confessions*, presented in the form of conversational prayer, model both the secular value that one ought to probe one's thoughts and actions—the unexamined life is not worth living, thank you, Plato—and also the religious belief that only in seeking God does one find oneself. Self-understanding arises in conversation with God. "Where, then," Augustine asks God, "do you diffuse what remains of you after heaven and hell have been filled?"[23] Where indeed? Augustine's answer: inside the human person.

In such conversation with God the believer does not, like the contemplative, dismiss the self, reach around the self for God, crush the self underfoot. Rather, the self of the believer comes to flower during the praise of God. According to the *Confessions*, once Augustine recognized God, welcomed God, and joined with others in praising God, Augustine's self opened up, making him better able to analyze his thoughts, probe his motives, understand his actions. The emotional, intellectual, and ethical chaos of Augustine's earlier years became ordered into fruitful prayer, creative theology, and service to his parishioners. The famous "rest" that the restless Augustine finds in God is not naptime, but a peace that enabled continued self-exploration and growth.

Augustine's conversational prayer became the model for much Christian free prayer in both the home and the church service. Many Protestants had rejected printed liturgical prayers as rote, as not coming truly from the heart, and they had also abandoned contemplative prayer, along with its monastic lifestyle, since the emerging capitalism in Christian countries afforded believers no time or space for mystical contemplation. Protestants wanted plenty of words, but ones freely chosen. And so Protestants were taught to "take it to the Lord in prayer" by talking daily with God, and even though the extemporized prayer in many Protestant churches can be almost rigidly formulaic, the syntax and vocabulary of the prayer mimics conversation.

I question people's claims that God has spoken to them, that Jesus has told them what to do today. That during meditation persons can get their act together and live more purposefully and peacefully afterward, I readily accept. That this was achieved by talking to God and God speaking back, I doubt. I do not say this has never happened: I doubt that it happens very often.

But mostly I doubt that one can be so sure: how does one come to assert that the morning's decision came from God? To me this sounds more like self-justification than faith. Did Augustine think that God told him not to marry his concubine? That's not what my God would have counseled. However, we do know that Augustine's intellectual framework, as well as his mother Monica, counseled against this marriage. Perhaps even so astonishingly self-analytical a person as Augustine confused the voice of mama with the voice of God. He would not be the first or last to do so. Unsure whether my inner voices—that superego that we used to call "conscience"—are mine, my culture's, my parents' or God's, I seldom try conversational prayer.

My daily praying is liturgical: a Celtic blessing upon waking; memorized meal prayers; a hymn, psalm, Bible reading, and intercessions shared with my husband after dinner; a prayer for the children, "for a quiet night and peace at the last," when curled up next to him in bed. I keep track of saints' days. My daughters report that when walking down the jetway they repeat the medieval prayer I taught them, that the angel Raphael will return us to our home "in health, in safety, and in joy." In all these practices my preference shows: pray with others, both the dead and the living; open myself to the next psalm, no matter what its topic or tone; rely on the tradition to place myself before God. It's not the popular American "Are you there God? It's me, Margaret," nor the eloquent Augustinian "What am I, when all is well with me, except one sucking your milk and feeding on you, the incorruptible food?"[24] But it will have to do.

If you can talk with God, go for it. I can't, quite, in that way. So in daily prayer, as in so many things, the rituals of traditional Christianity assist me, giving me a pattern I can step into, a path so well-worn that I am carried along in spite of myself. After nine chapters of Augustine's bifurcated, even tortured self-will, he relates his baptism at the Easter vigil in Milan with the minimalist sentence: "we were baptized." Pages and pages of "I" were edited down into the objective language of the liturgical "we." At least with the grand old formulas, I know I am opened up to past Christians and to the others currently praying these words. Who knows: perhaps I am opened also to God.

so we practice the faith

I have practiced the keyboard for thousands of hours. Beginning as a preschooler, I played through the red-covered John Thompson series with my mother as instructor. Some years later, I accompanied the hymns at my Lutheran school's morning devotions. By high school, I was studying at a nearby music conservatory. My father bought our family a eight-rank tracker organ (yes: amazing, isn't it?), and I practiced Bach trio sonatas on my way to becoming a church musician. But my rigorous hours at the keyboard ceased after college. Since, at the time, I was married to a pianist, the apartment was saturated with music, far better music than I could make, and I practiced silence.

Now my pianist-daughter is grown and gone, and the baby grand waits there silently. I walk by the shining black bulk. Should I play a Bach invention? the Mozart variations? a hymn? I walk past the piano, sit down on the sofa, and read. But I know that the piano is there, and even right now I could put down this pen (I write my books in longhand, with a pen on lined paper) and go practice again.

They say that once you learn to ride a two-wheeler, you never forget. I remember my dad running along behind the bike, urging me to pedal as fast as I talked. So you practice speed and learn balance, and then you can bike. And after twenty years, you straddle that frame and off you go, biking merrily down the street. But it's not like that with the piano: you gotta practice. Legs recall how to go around, but fingers don't seem to remember the distance between the keys or to retain the muscle control required to produce the desired sound.

Ritualizing religious faith is more like playing the piano than riding a bike. Oh, I know that old old persons who can't remember even their names can recite the Lord's Prayer. Yes, some things stay, perhaps, if they were early memorized and often repeated. But the Sunday liturgy and the Easter vigil and daily prayer, these require practice. On Easter Sunday morning I watch the annual visitors: clueless, they appear either disoriented or detached. They're very out of practice. And whenever I decide, once again, not to sit at the piano to relearn that Bach, I realize why, finally, someone so out of practice with Christian ritual simply gives it up altogether.

Part of the disillusionment many worshippers experience comes from an inaccurate expectation: they think of the Sunday event as something like a concert. I recall the New York premier of Krzysztof Penderecki's "St. Luke Passion." I knew that the world-famous composer had created a life-altering—perhaps religious—experience and that the symphony orchestra, each player a consummate performer, had rehearsed the complex score for weeks. All I had to do was sit there in the concert hall to be overwhelmed by the excellence of the superb performance. The conclusion of the piece found the audience so transported that moments of silence passed before the uproar of applause began. And then Penderecki himself came out on stage: there he was, here was the genius who had done it. The audience went berserk.

Some worshippers imagine that the church service is like this concert, that the preacher is the composer, that the organist and choir are the performers. Of course they are disappointed. In Christian ritual, the people in the pews are the performers, and the event is a rehearsal. We are all practicing the ritual, hoping to do it better this week than last.

Our culture grows increasingly impatient with practicing. Why concentrate on finger control for years when you can pop a CD into the player and hear perfect Bach, with the few errors made by the professionals having been electronically erased from the tape? Instant perfection is more appealing than practice, practice, practice. But I think most feminists would agree with me on this: practice by the whole group, not performance by a select few, is our ritual of choice. Society provides quite enough venues in which big shots make their money entertaining or edifying or horrifying us. And although megachurches are aping this pattern, the congregation relaxing in theater seats and watching a skit about Jesus, true religious ritual is different. In religious ritual, we enact our beliefs, as well as we can.

Of course religious ritual is practice: religious faith itself is practice. Together we try out the beliefs, we experiment with what they mean, we judge whether they work, we share stories of success and failure, we argue a bit or a lot, we say it a new way. It is hoped our skills improve.

Practice: In 1845 the Shaker Hannah Cohoon, who along with other women in the Hancock, Massachusetts, commune was receiving messages from Holy Mother Wisdom and recording them in spirit-drawings for the whole community to experience, painted a "Tree of Light, or Blazing Tree," each branch laden with leaves, each leaf tinged with tongues of flame. Later, Cohoon painted the much-reproduced Tree of Life, her masterpiece of green and orange flowers. But in 1996, Sotheby's was all aflutter with its find: a couple had bought a five-dollar frame at a yard sale, and under the print of an English hunting scene was a second Hannah Cohoon Blazing Tree, dated 1854.

Anyone who knows Cohoon's work immediately recognizes this tree as hers. Yet the differences between the earlier and later Blazing Tree are intriguing. The second is more diffuse; the gossamer branches are longer, the leaves fewer, each leaf thinner. One wonders if a decade of Shaker life had shown Cohoon that the fire of communal life was gentler than she had once imagined. The blaze is less intense. More air shows through the flames. Scholars of spirit-drawings might be perplexed: what about the theory that the Shaker women produced these drawings in nearly trance-like religious devotion? What we have here is at least a second try, perhaps even a woman practicing her tree-art to get it just right.

Practice: A popular Christian song these days is Michael Joncas' "On Eagle's Wings." The tune soars away, and we try like the notes to fly above our troubles. But I want the worshippers delighting in the refrain to know the biblical use of the image of eagle's wings. God pushes the Israelites out of Egypt, just as the mother eagle pushes the eaglets out of the nest, and they founder until in panic they figure out how to fly, but she coasts underneath them, to catch them on her wings if they fall. The image is not of successful flight: it's about practice. It's not the wealthy enjoying the Concorde, but the toddler learning balance.

Practice: It's like sex. You both get better and better at it. And you like to stay in practice, because it's different every time.

and ensuing ethics. . .

our goal is not heaven

Eastern and Western religions have imagined the afterlife in two quite different ways. In the East, the power of life gets reused over and over forever: an individual uses that power for a lifetime and then releases it back so it can become incarnate in yet another living creature. The West has imagined each individual person as having immortality. Traditionally Christians have assumed that one's everlasting consciousness will dwell with God in a place variously described but always called heaven. This Western idea of personal immortality was articulated by the upper classes of the ancient world. Surely, thought the Pharaoh of Egypt or the philosopher in Athens, I am too big a deal to be done with when I'm dead; surely at least the mighty ones will survive death. The Israelite version focused on sanctity: Enoch and Elijah were too holy to have suffered death on their way to be with God. In both East and West, the hierarchical triangle was essential to the afterlife. In the East, the triangle determined in which direction your life was headed for its next existence, up to the higher class or down toward the animals; in the West, the hope for an afterlife began with the guys on top and trickled down, until everyone, no matter how poor on earth, hoped to rise out of the muck and enjoy a royal lifestyle in heaven.

Faced squarely, the hope for immortality seems childish, an unwillingness among the privileged to face their end in death and a fantasy nursed by the lowly to inhabit a castle in the sky. But Christians have eagerly participated in these pervasive human desires. Medieval theologians said it was one's soul that would go back to God, since the soul—which was understood as the immortal part of a human being that came from God—would naturally revert to its source. Aquinas proposed some of the details of "ensoulment": a boy fetus gets its soul at six weeks' gestation, a girl fetus at twelve weeks', and at death the soul returns to the divine stasis of its Creator. Theologians suggested that the souls would be stationed closer or further from God depending on their degree of holiness. Not surprisingly, the virgin mystic Mechthild of Madgeburg asserted that the souls of female virgins would be closest to God in the great throne room of heaven.

121

Fra Angelico, however, painted monks dancing with angels, and so the fantasy got amplified: if we are to dance in heaven, our souls must have the capabilities of already resurrected bodies. By the nineteenth century, heaven was described as a spectacular gardened city filled with perfect Victorian families on perpetual vacation, a sort of summer camp over the rainbow. Some theologians taught that we would immediately know all divine mysteries, and others suggested that throughout eternity we would experience a continuous growth in God. Emmanuel Swedenborg, a renegade-Lutheran mystic, wrote that people who were spiritually immature and who had not listened attentively to sermons would begin in heaven as (you won't believe this) cats, but that, fear not, heaven provided everlasting opportunity for improvement.

On the heaven question, most of my students hold one of two opinions. Many, influenced by the Great American Religion, believe that all people will end up in heaven to enjoy a glorified anthropomorphic eternity. Others, mostly the smart science majors, find the teachings about heaven and an immortal soul to be wholly unbelievable, and a few report that since their religious training had promoted heaven as the primary if not the sole goal of religion, they have discarded God along with such prescientific descriptions of cosmology and personal immortality. To those people committed to ecological concerns, Christianity appears to promote a Platonic escape from nature, even while claiming that God created nature and pronounced it very good. The church, meanwhile, is doing little to provide a mature consideration of divine and human life, a reflection on life and death before God that accords with, rather than ignores, our contemporary understanding of reality. That a stellar list of twentieth-century theologians has downplayed or doubted or denied personal immortality—take for example Reinhold Neibuhr, Paul Tillich, Rudolf Bultmann, Karl Rahner, Dietrich Bonhoeffer, A.N. Whitehead, Rosemary Radford Ruether—has not affected the church's pastoral practice, which continues to talk in medieval terms about grandma's soul flying up to enjoy life with God in heaven.

It is not easy to let go of heaven. We Westerners want an everlasting personal consciousness. Christians have described the human self in its thinking, its loving, and its willing as the closest analogue we have to a personal God. Thus, we reason, as there is an eternal God, so must our souls be eternal. Indeed, some Christians have suggested that the capability of eternal life is what Genesis 1 means by the "image of God" that humans alone are granted.

I cannot recall how much my years of childhood catechesis stressed heaven. But by the time I was thirty, I no longer imagined that the walled royal park of ancient Persia was my final destiny. As a contemporary person, I rejected the idea that this life is only the narthex of our existence, that joy is promised us after death, that misfortune and pain and unhappiness are the price one pays to gain entry into the great banquet in the skies. My style of contemporary Christianity understands suffering as evil, as the enemy of all that is God, rather than as God's pop quizzes or semester exams.

What comes after me, says the believer, is God. So when I said to my father as he lay dying in the hospice, "Now you can go to God," what did I mean? I do not believe that my father is somewhere talking with the spirits of the dead, or that I will hug him again some day, however comforting that is to imagine. Rather, I believe that his death, like all deaths, like the death of Jesus, culminates with God. Christians need not be terrified of death, and we need not undergo heart transplants in our eighties. For me this life is all I have, but my life begins by God and ends with God. I understand that patients might be nervous about physician-assisted suicide, but I hope that by the time I am dying of terminal something, my Christian community has no problem with clergy-assisted suicide.

Without a heaven, Christian life can be more than with one. God gives this life, and it is precious beyond comprehension, more intense than every garden or city the poets can describe. If God is to be honored and praised, such worship must happen here, not after death above the clouds. No-heaven induces the ethical life: if all the world's people are to enjoy a plenteous banquet, we have scads of work to do to prepare the meal. The goal of religious faith is not life after death, but the transformation of this life by holiness and justice. For a feminist, the hierarchical triangle has flattened. Heaven is not up there for the good guys, the big shots; God, higher and deeper and more full of joy and more full of pain than we can say, is here. I need not desire an everlasting destiny in heaven, for the resurrection offers to us all a transformed life here, one already filled with God.

Over the years, several of my students have told me of their family tragedies involving infant death, their stories concluding with their confidence that the dead baby has become a guardian angel. I suppose the idea is that an infant, who never had a life that can climax in heaven, gets the compensatory reward of instant angelhood. I've heard that this belief is intensified by Baroque art, in which toddler cherubs circle around the saints. It's a religious myth that was never told us unfanciful Lutherans. Even as a child, I was taught that angels are angels and humans are humans; and what are dead humans? Surely not angels.

I did not tell my students my view that, sad but true, dead babies do not become angels, perhaps for the same reason that theologians do not announce at press conferences that there is no immortal soul. Instead I repeated the traditional Christian metaphoric phrase, that "light perpetual" may shine upon the one who has died, a prayer that means, at least, "May God be bigger than death." We use these images to help us believe. What holds together my dear students and the speculative theologians and me is the faith that there is God, that God is greater than we are, that life in God is more ultimate than the death of our selves.

The interior of the Lutheran cathedral in Helsinki, Finland, is as devoid of religious symbolism as was the rationalist piety that built it. Above the altar is its single depiction of the divine: a deposition, the body of the dead Jesus being removed from the cross. Looking at the lifeless Christ, one might assume that religion is about the moments after death, about where we will be carried when we get taken off our cross. For such a spirituality, a literal heaven of personal bliss is essential. But happily not for me.

but justice in the arena

An hour from Philadelphia is Lancaster County, home to one of the world's largest Amish settlements. On the back roads one sees their farms, the black bonnets on the women, the signs announcing their cottage industries—"Quilts for Sale, Never on Sunday." Incongruously, the main highway through Amish country is now lined with monstrous discount malls. So within a mile, sitting in your car, you wait behind a buggy turning left, and then you wait for that one parking space in a lot the size of a farm.

For the bonneted women, Christian ethics is obedience. The whole of their baptized life funnels through the Household Codes, those passages in the epistles directing each wife to obey her husband, children their father, and slaves their master. The German word that the Amish use is *Gelassenheit*, submission to God, to the authority of the elders, to the will of the community, to everyone higher than you in the chain of command. An Amish question-and-answer book asks what happens if a husband is unworthy of his wife's obedience. The unequivocal answer: "No matter."[25] Her task is still obedience. Amish children are taught the acronym JOY: Jesus first, Others next, Yourself last. Perhaps in a community as tight as the Amish, the life of obedience is more gift than burden. If you must submit, you might as well choose to.

It takes half my heart away, thinking of the Christian women who were taught that baptism necessitates obedience, but who could never be on the top of the obedience chain. Only their children and the farm animals were below them. History shows that many such obedient women became skilled in manipulating their way around, excelling in the subterfuge cultivated by subjugated persons. Hardly an ethical paradise.

Many American Christians have been raised in an obedience ethic not dissimilar to that of the Amish. Transplanted from medieval Europe, where God and the dominant men stood arm-in-arm, is the ethics of the old boring hierarchical pyramid, in which the many on the bottom must sit nice and still so as to provide solid support for the few sitting on top of them. I see in many students an acceptance of the life of obedience: obey your parents and teachers, God likes obedience and punishes disobedience. Some students claim that Jesus always obeyed his mother, for they are unaware of the several gospel narratives that indicate his detachment from—if not disregard for—her. One part of me is pleased when students contest their grade, for they so rarely challenge authority.

But complicating my students' consciousness is the American concentration on self-fulfillment. Unaware as yet of the self's insatiability, they speak of their hope for a life of happiness determined by the self, limited only by the self. So what happens when we realize that an ethical system based on obedience contradicts a contemporary self-fulfillment credo? When religion does not support cultural values and only sets up static, one solution is to turn down the religion. I see the conflict on their young faces and read it in their ingenuous papers.

On the other hand, as a feminist Christian, I offer Perpetua, the first renowned female Christian martyr. A 22-year-old noblewoman, newly married, nursing her newborn, she was arrested, interrogated, imprisoned, and thrown to the beasts in the arena in northern Africa in perhaps 203 C.E. Her memoir describes her ordeal and relates her visions. A witness to her martyrdom completed the narrative.

Here's an ethical proposal inspired by Perpetua: Far from confiscating your will, religion strengthens your self-identity. Perpetua's Christianity gave her self-determination. Along with many other Christian women whose biographies nurture me, Perpetua was rendered more feminist by her religion. Her faith empowered her to live free from patriarchy, to make independent decisions, to bond with a voluntary community over against her natural family. She disobeyed her father, she gave up her newborn son for adoption—not a good mommy—and she broke the law, peacefully accepting the grim outcome. In the description of her visions, she tells of a serpent lurking at the base of a ladder she must climb, and she steps on its head to ascend. In the garden of Eden, God predicts that someone will crush the head of the serpent. Apparently Perpetua knew that the "someone" was every believer. She envisions drinking sweet milk, surrounded by thousands in white robes. I hope that before her death, as she was nursing, she tasted her breast milk and so knew her own sweetness.

Perpetua knew that Christian ethics is not about being nice. Rather, it is about the resurrection, about the transformation of humankind. It is about the explosion of life through rock, the fusion of disparate elements into a *novum* that rearranges the periodic table. Anthropologists speculate that humans first placed huge stones over a buried body to ensure that the dead would stay dead and the spirit would remain captive underground. Ha! says the resurrection. I will arise, to step on your toes, or perhaps even your head, as I ascend my confident new life.

It is the conservative in us that relies on rules and enforces the rules, fearful that only the old way is trustworthy. Christian ethics can break through the rules since it believes that in God we can do a new thing, and that the new thing can be good.

It's understandable that an ethics emanating from monotheism could espouse obedience. The One is on top of the pyramid, and I appear to be close to the bottom, and so's I better sit still and keep my hands in my pockets. But Christian ethics flows from the Trinity, who is a Three-in-One, a three-petaled flower, a three-figured dance, an illogical equation. One-in-Three must discover a new way to fit. Christian theology maintains that the three persons of the Trinity are co-equal: this breaks the expected pattern of how three might inter-relate. One-in-Three reconfigures the design. Three-in-One encircles us. We are holding hands.

As a Christian, my ethical questions must be triune. First, what is it today that I am to create? Second, what today, besides myself, needs to be pulled back from the grave? And, third, what group is waiting for me today, holding a place for me in the circle? "One is our God who creates, saves, and cares," I wrote in a children's number book. Well, if the Trinity, then the Christian: creating, saving, caring. The list of what needs creating, saving, and caring begins easily enough. There's my husband, my daughters, my extended families, my friends, my stu-dents, my colleagues, my manuscripts. But I am grabbed by Perpetua, whose list omitted all the my's. "I am a Christian," she announced, and, disregarding the usual list, she headed toward the beasts.

Perpetua's death was and was not justice in the arena. It was not justice that at twenty-two she be killed for refusing an action so consummately stupid as sac-rificing to the emperor. Yet by her execution she enacted a justice beyond herself, trading her own life for a divine spirit of rebellion that would nurture the com-munity. We obsessively individualistic sorts will find this justice troublesome to emulate. But let's be honest: the chances that I will ever be asked to follow Perpetua to death are minuscule. In much of my life, I need not be the rule-breaker, because I am the rule-maker. I design the syllabus and determine the grades; I choose where to contribute my tithe; I decide in which companies to invest my pension; I control the books I write, the countries I visit. As a tenured Westerner, buying a week's groceries with the money I can earn in an hour, I am not oppressed or helpless.

Although it would be disingenuous for me to pretend that because some women are thrown into the arena, I am, I must always be joining at least my con-sciousness with those who are. I ought neither deny my privileged position nor disregard the misery of those whose lives are lessened by my privilege. Although I am in the socio-economic situation to sit in the stands, indeed, to have organized the event, both feminist consciousness and Christian ethics impel me to transmigrate from spectator—perhaps even perpetrator—to victim. Dorothy Day lived with the victims: I must at least imagine their life.

So, trusting that our community can become the embodiment of the Spirit of God, we enact a justice that has far more to do with the resurrection than with rules. But, the truth is, we must struggle to see the design of the resurrection. There is a feminist fantasy that when we are all sitting in a circle under a tree, there will be no more quarreling, no more need for authority, no more desire for power. Yet my studies of nineteenth-century Philadelphia Quaker life suggest quite the opposite: that people are unruly whether they sit in a line or a circle, and that without clear ordering, a community gets instead endless dissension over who gets to talk how long. Discerning the Spirit requires labor. Many contemporary Christians prefer not to call God judge: yet trinitarian ethics would, it seems, require lots of judging on our part, plenty of expertise in the knowledge of good and evil, many decisions about what constitutes justice.

Perpetua must have emanated authority. Females thrown to the beasts were dressed up as devotees of the goddess Ceres, yet she refused. She'd die in her own Christian clothes, thank you very much. And when first tossed into the air and her hair became disheveled, she asked for a barrette to pin it up. The point is: to enact justice you have to have your self together. My one self must cultivate dual capabilities, both overseeing the situation and suffering under its cruelties. It means leading the line while forming a circle. It means discerning when to use my position and when to vacate it.

care for the trees

This week, as I write, autumn is climaxing in Philadelphia. Even taking out the garbage borders on a religious experience. The Japanese maple is ruby red, the locust still jade, the northern red oak already jasper, the tulip tree an amber glow, the burning bush a garnet horde—although I think it was actually a transplanted sugar maple that Moses saw on that mountain when he claimed that in the tree was God, shining a fiery gold. But I must admit that a comparison with gems is inadequate, for leaves are more alive than jewels. On some single leaves is the entire autumn rainbow, every color except the blue of the backdrop sky, while other leaves are only one solid color apiece, like cards of color swatches in a New England paint store.

Although I grew up adoring autumn, imagining all the Connecticut trees to be wearing the colors of my wardrobe, I did not come early to concern for the trees. I took in the trees with my eyes, yet kept an urban distance from their care. I wasn't much good at walks in the woods: too hot for my fair skin in summer, too cold for my poor circulation in winter. So I admit coming an hour late to the ethics of ecology and to a decent pair of hiking shoes.

I came to care for living trees because I first cared for the tree of life. Metaphor pulled me into matter. The images of mythically magical and psychically extraordinary trees in the art in our house, in the museums I visit, and in the religions I study finally focused my attention on the trees in our yard, the trees by the Maine coast, the rainforests upon which our life depends. Such is the power of metaphor, to make us see newly. Metaphor had accomplished its miracle; it transmogrified the commonplace into the splendid.

Other influences prodded me along. My husband backpacks in the woods, my daughters developed a passion for recycling. I encountered wicca's retrieval of the ancient pantheistic concept of divinity: what is alive is what is divine, and we are to honor nature as the goddess she is. Starhawk's tree-of-life ritual expresses this well: we are rooted in divinity, and we bring forth the divine until at death we merge back into a holy matrix. Recently Starhawk has written, no longer of the masculine as destructive, but of the natural balance between masculine and feminine as emblematic of the divine powers required for the continuing life of the universe.

Some Christian theologians, coming onto the green scene, are using the word panentheism to articulate why we are to honor the earth without divinizing it. Gone are the days when the church can adopt a patronizing tone and cite from Genesis an autocratic command to subdue the earth. Rather, panentheism understands that although God is not identified as the natural universe, God is revealed within it. The universe is in God: thus God is in the universe. For trinitarian Christians, divine incarnation did not begin and end with the life of Jesus. Rather, God's self-revelation, begun in the creation of the world and manifest in Christ, continues by God's Spirit throughout the world. Sally McFague, for example, extends traditional religious language by calling all creation the body of God.

Two theologians, one a Roman Catholic woman and one a Lutheran man, have recently written prize-winning books dealing with panentheism. Elizabeth Johnson, schooled in Thomism and living in a women's community, speaks of the life-giving aspect of panentheism. The world is like the growing infant within the womb of mother God; the mutual participation of God and the world is like a feminist ideal of friendship—"each indwelling the other,"[26] yet free. Meanwhile, Larry Rasmussen, in the tradition of Martin Luther and Dietrich Bonhoeffer, writes of the hidden God, the divine surprisingly discovered in the finitude of earth. Humans come from humus—"the organic residue of roots, bone, carrion, feces, leaves"[27]—and we encounter God within the living and dying of all that is natural and mortal.

I, a woman and a Lutheran, smile: I'll take them both. I am glad to see God's life in the resplendent autumn trees, but as I watch the nurseryman take down a grand tree which they say was diseased—although we see no trace of that in the cross sections of its trunk lying discarded on the lawn—I know the death of life. I care for the trees not only because, finally, I realize that their life is part of the I-who-I-are. Panentheism proposes that while there is a reality more ultimate than the trees, this ultimate mystery is borne by my beloved autumn leaves. Our honoring God impels us to honor the forest, in which is God.

Genesis says that after the fall an angel guarded the way to the tree of life, forbidding humans access to its divine power. Adam was sent out "to till the ground from which he was taken." Early theologians maintained that without sin humans would have been immortal—a misunderstanding of the myth that strikes us as not only pretentious but even ludicrous. The tree of life, denied us because of sin, was to be ours only after death, in heaven's magnificent garden with eternally ripe orchards. "Tilling the ground" came to refer solely to acquiring and accumulating one's own food, as if we were to care for the soil only because we needed to eat its fruits.

There is still power in this legend, but only with a far different interpretation, under a greener light. When the youngest child asks what it means to be human, we can answer: Well, we are creatures who come to distinguish good from evil, who learn to recognize the difference between God's divinity and our own mortal naked hungry sexual selves. The Eden legend is about growing up, about getting dressed and going to work, about admitting that happiness doesn't grow on magical trees, about our obligation to care for the matrix. The childhood fantasy of eternal life is over. The story shows our life as the human participation in the natural world that God created: we till the ground from which we come. God puts us in a treed land where both fruits and rot abound. The Christian ethical life calls us to be in this world as in a place filled with God, to keep its life flowing, to put on a sweater rather than turning up the furnace, to plant a tree each year.

I have always been irritated by nineteenth-century poetry in which death was just marvelous because we all end up daffodils. I prefer the image of the nurse-log. A nurse-log is a decaying log from a dead tree which provides the nutrients for a living tree. The young tree grows upright out up from the log lying spent on the ground. But here's the Christian part: the nurse-log is Christ, God's stark way to be with us most fully within the living, dying world. And here's the Christian ecological part: the forest is not other than us, and not apart from the God who made us.

bedrooms that benefit the body

I n the last semester of college, we honors students took a religion seminar with the university president. Sitting in rows in his dark office on velvet padded wooden chairs, we wore, if you can believe it, Sunday clothes, dresses and nylons, suits and ties. His considerable girth hidden behind his massive desk, he pontificated about this and that, but all I recall is his suggestion of the two four-letter words that characterized the differences between our lives and his: the bomb and the pill. He was a wise man. Perhaps it has been the bomb, either as the threat of total annihilation or as the daily chronicle of yet more random violence, that has clouded people's clarity about the future. And surely he was right about the pill, the contraceptive technology that separated in practice, not merely in theory or fantasy, sexual intercourse from childbearing and thus altered the world on which Christian sexual ethics reflects.

Thirty years have elapsed. Some Christians judge that contraception itself is a sin, the devil's way to circumvent God's sexual ethic. Other Christians inwardly condemn premarital sex while outwardly inviting for family festivals their adult children and live-in lovers. Many young people raised in mainstream Christian churches are bouncing from bed to bed, alternating moments of joy with hours of misery in a chaos of emotions that as a virgin I never even imagined. Some church leaders avoid these issues, unsure of what to say, unwilling to participate in the battles that ensue, while others preach a traditional ethic that has practically no resonance with people's actual experience. Thus, many contemporary Christians are left with no ethical guidance whatsoever, save their weekly attendance at the movie theater with its recurring message that a blissful bed awaits each of us every evening, with spouse or stranger, no matter.

Christians were ethically unprepared for the pill. Most of us had been taught that God approved, even established, one sex ethic: sexual intimacy was sinful outside of marriage yet—depending on your ethnic community or your denomination—either tolerated or wondrous within. That the Bible records as divinely sanctioned two contradictory sex ethics, polygamy and monogamy, was generally downplayed. Although my denomination had for some decades accepted contraception within marriage, and while my parents modeled the goodness of sexual intimacy, the biological core of Augustinianism held fast: sexual intercourse was essentially about babies and so belonged in marriage. The medieval world taught that God's reason for creating sexuality was procreation, and this message was passed down from mother to daughter: truth to tell, sex always ends up being about babies. In theory or practice, the sex ethic did not get much deeper than this one dimension. So when, as a college senior, my erratic menstrual cycle was medically regulated with the pill and I was for a time infertile, my sex ethic was bankrupt, unable to cover the new situation when sex no longer equalled babies.

Christian theologians offered various religious arguments in defense of this set-up: since sex equals babies, sex equals marriage. But we know that this ethic also derives logically from the economic arrangement common to patriarchal societies. The men own things, things like the means of survival. As well, they own the women, more or less, and a man hopes to control what he values most in the woman, which is her ability to reproduce. The father does not want his daughter to reproduce, since the baby is not his and yet he must support it; the husband does want his wife to reproduce, since the child will add to his wealth. In a culture in which males controlled the means of survival, this allocation of each woman to some man benefitted also the woman, who was assured that if she obeyed the rules, someone would feed her as she nursed and reared her child.

This is no longer our pattern. The glue that held this gizmo together has dried up. Our culture no longer thinks that males have biological, legal, and moral control of their offspring. Women select their own sexual partners and contract their own marriages: thus the incongruity of weddings in which the father "gives his daughter away." Some women are economically viable on their own, some so successfully that they can rear children and make money at the same time, and many other women aspire to such self-sufficiency. But central to the demise of this system is effective birth control, perhaps the single most significant plank in the platform of women's liberation. Thanks to relatively foolproof contraception, sexual intimacy need no longer be connected to the economics of child rearing, since sex no longer equals babies.

Many women are delighted with the new situation. But other women have fallen into the fissure with neither system sustaining them, for their sexual activity did in fact produce a baby, and no one is there to support them. What enrages me about the recent stories of teenage mothers killing their newborns are the quotes from the judges, the "I just can't imagine how she could have done such a thing" comments. Well, I can. Don't get mushy about mothers: infanticide was probably the only solution she could envision. What staggers me is only that no one else knew, that no one recognized her pregnant walk, that no one heard the labor cries, that no other person had confirmed with her and accompanied her into the reality of the coming child.

Feminist Christians have ahead the mammoth task of constructing a contemporary Christian sex ethic that recognizes the end of the patriarchal system. I do not find it comfortable to establish one ethic in my mind and yet tolerate a different ethic in my daily life. I want to say more to my daughters than "I don't know; good luck."

So I have come this far: to say that sexual activity has three different potencies, one for the self, one for the partner, and one for the offspring. That is: in the first place, sexual activity expresses and creates power in the self. It might be wholesome power, making me a deeply contented and emotionally focused person. Or it may be destructive: my sexual life may diminish me, render me afraid, tear me apart, make me more cruel, more wasteful of others. But one way or other, sexual activity will change me.

Secondly, sexual activity expresses and creates a bond between the partners. The bond might be wholesome. As the phrase "to make love" suggests, intimacy can generate more commitment between the partners. I can come to honor my partner more and discover that such honoring improves the world. The honoring will enliven, deepen, and gladden the partner. Experience teaches that—some say more for women than for men—sexual intimacy wants a future between the couple. A good principle seems to be: no future for the bond, no sex. However, the connection may be destructive. It may solidify domination, it may enact violence, it can handcuff life to decay. Those who are promiscuous disregard the power of this bonding, acting as if sex is only momentary coupling and nothing more.

Thirdly, then, at least for heterosexuals, there is the potentiality of offspring, sometimes a happy conception, sometimes a wretched surprise. But thanks to the pill, this third potency is no longer either an inevitable or—sorry, Augustine—the fundamental meaning of the action. And so, of course, contraception ushers in lesbian and gay rights, for even heterosexual Christians cannot pretend any more that their sexual activity is meant for procreation. When a baby does come, Christian ethics must ask not only after its economic survival, but also its psychological well-being, and we must judge the relative necessity of two parents, or one parent of each sex, or the biological parents themselves, for the wholesome rearing of offspring.

For curiosity I looked back through my copy of Dietrich Bonhoeffer's *Ethics*, for it was while studying this in college that I first went on the pill. I see now how christological Bonhoeffer's thinking is. In Christ is our life, and within Christ's mercy lie our ethical struggles. Bonhoeffer makes individual rights key to his ethical proposal, arguing that in creation and through the incarnation God has validated the freedom of the individual person. His logic strikes me as not distant from a Western secular affirmation of the inviolability of the individual, which feminists have used to claim for themselves their sexual powers.

The focus on individual rights will help us a little. Yes, a woman owns her own sexuality and should direct its use to benefit her body. One hopes that she is able to think like an adult before trying to act like one. I judge that most adolescent sex is unfortunate, sometimes destructive, sometimes disastrous. It crams one of the greatest adult potentialities into the small space of the teenager: either the sex gets quashed, or the youth explodes.

For it is clear that sexual activity does not necessarily benefit one's body. And I am thinking not only of rape, but of the many ways that sexual activity is a commodity paid out for some exchange, with the price seldom, it seems, having been calculated correctly. The bartering leads to loss. If Augustine held that, except for babies, sex always expressed sinful lust, the movies suggest the opposite, that, babies now out of the picture, sex always promises personal happiness. The hope that sexual potency ought to benefit the self meets the reality that it often does not.

I must, however, go beyond Bonhoeffer's individual rights. Like so many male theologians in the Christian tradition, Bonhoeffer got as far as Christ and stopped, content with the language that God meets "man" in the incarnation. I join with the feminist Christians who are more trinitarian. Just as God's life is a dance in three, a balance within the commune, so the life of the Christian community is realized around God and within the community. Christian ethics must inquire not only what is my right, but what will benefit the community. Christian ethics pushes me toward not the mirror but the other. The issue is not what I can do for me, but what we can do for one another, for in meeting the other we meet God.

We quickly recognize the limitations of grounding our sexual ethic in individual rights when we consider current reproductive technologies. Lesbians can be artificially inseminated, and women can be impregnated with embryos from strangers. If we approach these moral inquiries attending solely to individual rights, we end up in confusion. We are rightly nervous about granting approval, for we know that coming round the bend is the issue of the rights of the child, its right to know its parents, to see them together, to grow connected with its own history. We had better ask about the rights of the genetic parents, when eventually both the mother and the father awaken to their obligations as givers of life. We wear ourselves out, juggling one person's rights over another's.

We must think of sexual ethics as benefitting the body of at least the couple. Paul taught that in intercourse the two bodies become one and, in a passage remarkably egalitarian for a first-century author, that the husband and the wife bear equal authority over the body of the other. I'd say it differently: that the husband and the wife each share equal potency towards the ecstasy of the other. Thus, every situation of sexual intimacy—whether involving children, adolescents, adults, single persons, a married couple, heterosexuals, homosexuals—must face the inquiry: is this intimacy benefitting the body that is made in the coupling? Once more, it's not the I, but the I-who-I-are.

Unfortunately, we are often mistaken about whether an activity will benefit our singular or plural body. When in the garden of Eden the serpent says, "You will be like gods," the "you" is plural. The woman was choosing a life for the couple, but, just as with everyone who has ever lived, what she thought would be an improvement turned into trouble. The artist Naomi Limont depicts this in her print of Eden: Eve and Adam are standing between two immense trees, but it is not clear which one is the tree of life.

And we can't stop with this already difficult inquiry into the body of the couple. There is also the body of the community. The I-who-I-are includes not only my beloved one, but also my family, my beloved's family, our neighbors, our associates. As Augustine suggested by his trinitarian language of God as Lover, the Beloved, and Love, the offspring of the bond between the Lover and the Beloved is Love, a third of equal strength and beauty. The truth is that sexual relations do not remain private, enclosed within the couple. The intimacy shows; the potency extends its powers; there is that third dimension. To keep sexual intimacy a secret requires of the couple gargantuan effort and considerable deception, for the tight bond naturally springs out into the wider community. I hope that sooner rather than later the church blesses homosexual unions: for I have seen homosexuals careen from one emotional disaster to another, and I have witnessed homosexual couples sharing a home and a life, enriching the society with their steady resolve to care and commitment, and it is clear that the second of these arrangements is better for the entire community than the first. I am not pretending that marriage guarantees stability, but I know that the body of any couple benefits from the support of the body of the community in the hopefully endless undertaking of love.

Despite its patriarchal context, there is one biblical story that illustrates a sexual ethic for the community. The Israelite widow Naomi and her foreign daughter-in-law Ruth are left alone to fend for themselves, because the family's young men, whose names translate "sickness" and "consumption," have died. Naomi concocts a plan to get Ruth remarried, and it involves Ruth's spending the night at the town's threshing floor, where no self-respecting woman belongs, and uncovering Boaz's feet, which a bold commentary will tell you probably meant, as it often did in ancient Hebrew narrative, his genitals. Ruth ends up married to Boaz; Naomi, miraculously, nurses the baby; and the child grows up to be the grandfather of King David. The patriarchal sexual ethic of the time, as well as the religious requirement that the Israelite Boaz refrain from marrying the Moabite Ruth, have given way to the exigencies of these two proto-feminists, whose decisions about sex brought about joy and prosperity for the whole Israelite people. One could say that Naomi, disregarding several ethical principles along the way, conceived a bedroom that benefitted the entire body.

In the village of Lowthorpe, England, behind the pews in the small stone church, brought inside to be protected from the weather, is the fourteenth-century tomb cover for Thomas and Alice Heslerton. In many medieval churches one sees stone effigies of married couples, the noblewoman and nobleman laid out side by side in all their elegant finery. This tombstone is different. The couple is covered up to their necks as if with a blanket, and on the blanket is a great tree, and on its branches like fruits are the heads of their many children.

I hope that Alice and Thomas loved each other as much as this stunning tombstone suggests. And whenever I look at the tree-of-life quilt on my marriage bed, I hope that the ecstacy of our bed will nurture life, not merely for me, not merely for us, but for all. But I cannot forget that this bedroom is my second try at marriage, one tree cut down for another one to grow. Probably it happens seldom that one's bedroom, from beginning to end, benefits the whole body, from beginning to end. But such seems to me the Christian ethical goal for the sexual potency of the I-who-I-are.

for we all are the body

I n a patriarchal culture, like much of the Roman empire, an individual's value is determined by the relation of that person to the patriarch. Value trickles down from the *paterfamilias* to the slave girl under his roof. Were she a beautiful young woman, however, and noticed by the patriarch, her value might suddenly change. It is clear from first- and second-century documents, written both by and about the early Christian movement, that this emerging religion recognized within its membership, and sought throughout the wider society, a re-evaluation of persons. Christians proclaimed that God loves each individual, God saves each person. The New Testament contains many stories of persons for some reason without social value—a poor widow, a woman accused of adultery, a condemned criminal, a child—who are singled out for God's blessing. One sees why the story of Jesus came to be called "good news." Patriarchs are few: the vast numbers of the nameless poor and dispossessed, whose only social importance is to provide the foundation for the patriarchal palace, are delighted to hear that though their ruler may dismiss their worth, the great God honors them.

This Christian message—God's honoring of each person—has been enthusiastically received in Western culture. At least in the United States, perhaps the single most pervasive article of societal faith is the equal value of each individual. Of course, equality is not yet, and probably never will be, a social reality. Each nation has its oppressed class or color, but in the West even those people tend to believe that although they aren't being treated equally, they ought to be. We read with disbelief of a Mauritanian woman telling a Western reporter that God created her to be a slave. And so it is that far too many gay teenagers commit suicide when they confront the disparity between their belief in being equal and the reality of their being ostracized. And although Greek philosophy taught that it was especially one's soul that had value, recent American thought lauds the physical body. "Our bodies, ourselves" informs Socrates that I am my body and that my body has value equal to anyone's: I deserve a heart transplant, if anyone does.

But as my husband-theologian teaches, to speak truthfully of God one must always say two things. One sentence cannot contain all the truth: a contrasting sentence is required as well. For example, Christians say that the bread is the body of Christ and that the community is the body of Christ. Neither sentence is complete without the other sentence correcting it, expanding it, illuminating it. And so one Christian truth—God values everybody—needs balance by a second sentence: we all are the body. In Christianity the one God is three, and this Trinity calls us to be one in community. Yes, God loves me, but I am the I-who-I-are.

Take for example abortion. A patriarchal system condemns abortion as denying the father his property, since the baby is understood as the product of his sperm. One Christian voice teaches that because God loves especially the helpless fetus, we are required to give the child its life. A secular feminist might say that the pregnant woman owns her own body and so can choose how that body is to be fruitful. Each of these three positions argues the priority of one individual over all others.

As a Lutheran, I was taught that in everything we are sinners. It is evil to kill in war; however, it is also evil to ignore oppression and allow the helpless to suffer. So I must consider when even the birth of a child is more an evil for the mother, perhaps for the community, than not. I do not consider a fertilized egg to be an instant human person; indeed, our culture does not mourn as dead children the twenty to forty percent of all pregnancies that terminate in spontaneous miscarriage. Since the fourth century, most of us Christians are not pacifist: our ethics exonerates men for their taking of life in war. It is time for also women to be granted immunity, as they help one another judge what loss is necessary for life.

But when a woman in my congregation announced early on an unwanted pregnancy—the conception having marked the last time she slept with her estranged husband—and all of us were counseling her about the coming child and her abandoned marriage, her eventual and late abortion seemed to me the death of an infant member of our community. Yet what is my sense of outrage beside the tragedy of that woman's life? It is clear that I have no simple formula for abortions. Christian ethics, however, provides no simple formulas. To love one's neighbor as oneself? This only begins the inquiry.

I suggest that a feminist Christian ethic would move beyond quarreling over which individual wins the day. Not the father's right, not the fetus's right, not the mother's right: rather, what is best for the community? Thinking trinitarianly, we would consider both the hopes and the limits of the wider community: the infant's life, its health and well-being, the mother's health and livelihood, the situation of the father and his ability to care for his child, the other children, their care and nurture, who knows what else. We listen to the entire matrix appealing to us. Of course, the ethical decision will now be more difficult to make. It is simpler to know what I want, or to imagine what some single individual wants, than to be wise about the complex needs of an entire community.

That we all are the body is the theme of the Christian sacrament of the eucharist. The idea is that God is in Christ, and that Christ is in a body, and that his body is in this bread, and that this bread is consumed by this community; and so God is alive in this community. There is a new communion custom spreading around in which the minister calls each communicant by name: "The body of Christ for you, Suzie." While this is well-meaning, perhaps personally significant for some, certainly a nightmare for ministers who blank on first names, it is a notable departure from historic Christian meaning, and we'd best think twice about it. The "you" in the biblical passages that the phrase cites is a plural you. The body of Christ comes to the community together, not to me privately. The cup of life is not a jiggerful of health for me, a shot of holy joy juice. Rather, it's shared food in the body of the community. In the Middle Ages, some communicants sought to take the bread home with them, to revere in a household shrine, or to plant in the garden for good luck. So the clergy were required to place the host into the communicant's mouth. You had to eat it here. This is the body, this group, consuming this food together. It's not magic for me, but a meal for us.

But here's the next But. We can't think of the body as Leonardo de Vinci's perfect naked male outstretched over the globe, a flawless man in beautiful proportion and exquisite form. Nor is the body the magnificent matron Wisdom, her majesty exemplifying natural excellence. Let's get real: the body, like every body we know, is imperfect, mortal, parts of it dying, parts still coming to be. Here is an image of the body: a nineteenth-century Kansas settler, waking at midnight during a blizzard, her menstrual blood having soaked through all the rags she brought with her in the covered wagon, as well as through their one large sheet and the straw mattress, and she discovers that the bucket of water is frozen solid, and the frigid stream is a several minute walk from the sodhouse: what did that woman do? But here's the good news: she—her body—made it. The woman survived into old age, saw six of her ten children grown to adulthood, and having taught them all to read out of the family Bible, was pleased that her eldest daughter became the first teacher in the county's one-room school.

The body that we are is not the ideal, but the actual. This is not a comforting truth. I want to be part of a grand figure, a matchless organism. I wish the church were the perfected embodiment of the Spirit of God. Yes, then Christian ethics would be fun, all of us working faultlessly as one. But this whole body is flawed, partial. As Annie Dillard wrote, "Nothing could more surely convince me of God's unending mercy than the continued existence on earth of the church."[28] This odd crew is the body of Christ. Like the historic Jesus—a baby born, a simple life, an execution, but no decaying corpse—we are a body victim to all the vagaries of natural life, yet somehow, we believe, victorious over death.

A Methodist minister tells that when distributing the wine he calls out, "The blood of Christ, the cup of salvation," and that once a communicant looked him in the eye and said, "I'll take the cup of salvation, thank you." Yes, we'd rather have the clear wine than the sticky blood. I'd rather think by myself about goodness than join together with you all in endless ethical struggles. But I am no anchorite; daily before us are communal ethical decisions. Sometimes we'll get it all wrong, buckets of blood all over the place. But we trust in divine mercy, for us and for everyone else, trying not to forget that, now that we are the body of Christ, we are to be the locus of that mercy for one another.

such is the religion of one
feminist Christian

I n these essays I might have presented a simpler definition of religion. For example, here's one: religion is a shared symbol system that gives meaning to life in the face of death.

A shared symbol system: I was raised in an especially conservative branch of an already conservative denomination, and my teachers cared devoutly, persistently, even fanatically, that we believe what is right. My Lutheran training wanted not only one's hands and heart to be religious, but one's brain as well, and so the intellect was integral to faithful observance. Lots of energy was and still is expended in disseminating theological journals in which a group of friends serves up a certain slice of the Lutheran pie as the best, perhaps the only, piece.

To keep doctrine graspable, God has to be relatively contained, the church controlled. So I am used to hearing people screech at each other, "What! You claim that you're Lutheran, after you said that about this?" Horrors! Did you hear her on the atonement, or pronouns for God, or sex ethics? I have witnessed bishops standing at microphones at a church convention close to tears as they presented their side of hugely controverted minutiae. In response they were informed that their reflections were "not to be tolerated within the church of God." Condemnations catapulted about. The cross becomes a crossbow. This is to say: I know that people want, need, to share a symbol system and that they can care passionately that the symbols cohere in logic and beauty, grounding us in the past and supporting us into the future.

For my adult life I have joined also the feminist search for shared symbols. And I know that while I have riled lots of the old boys, I have also disappointed some of the women, for we women do not yet agree on the name of God, the meaning of Christ, the life of the church. We examine the tree and diagnose its diseases differently, disagreeing which branches need to be removed lest the entire tree rot. Oh, it bites, it stings: the symbols fly around, elusive. We don't yet have

142

all the birds of the air finding refuge in our branches. *Half the Kingdom,* a video that surveys Jewish feminists, highlights one Orthodox feminist who describes her situation: the Orthodox condemn her as too feminist, and the feminists dismiss her as too Orthodox. At the conclusion of the film, two Jewish women, this Orthodox feminist and a radical critic of traditional Judaism, sit together in a kosher kitchen trying to talk with one another, acknowledging, if not one another's symbol system, at least one another.

There is a Kabbalist legend that in presenting to the Israelites the word from God, Moses first brought down from Sinai a tablet made from the tree of life on which were recorded all the names of God. This tablet ended up smashed. The second tablet he brought down was made from the tree of knowledge of good and evil and included all the rules for religious life. I like to imagine religion as a tree of life, but I am well aware that this religion is constructed of the tree of knowledge. The shared symbol system doesn't beam down from God, offering immediate fruits and granting peaceful shade. No, we have to tend it, prune it, prop it up here and there, protect it from tree-eating beetles. A parable in the gospel of Luke tells of a landowner who wanted to chop down an unproductive fig tree. No, pleaded the gardener: let's give it some manure for a year. So we all shovel away, those of us who are feminists and those who are not, hoping that some of our efforts will fertilize healthy growth.

A book about religion that uses the word "I" as much as did this one must account for itself. For characteristically, Christians have claimed that their religion comes from God. It was revealed by the divine, and one's I has nothing to do with it. Karl Barth, one of the twentieth century's preeminent theologians, taught that Christianity is not a religion, not a human symbol system at all, since it is a divine gift, God's grace an antidote to the poison of religion.

Barth is right about this: it is God, not religion, that saves. But thanks to our growing self-awareness, and to at least momentary humility, most of us no longer pretend that our views are objective or our religion's pronouncements divine. My thoughts arise in me; there is no scholarship, and no religion, that is disinterested. The self is always there, in my ears, in my mind, as well as in the words I choose. Even when saying the word God, the self is never absent. Yet we hope, I no less than Barth, that our words are not merely descriptions of ourselves, gilded mirrors in fancy frames.

We aim for symbols that are shared. The mirror reflects back a crowd. So while I claim the I in my religious devotion, I balance it by going to church each Sunday and by reading what others are writing. The theories of my mind, the play of my emotions, the hopes in my imagination, these meet the discipline of my butt in the pew and my nose in your book. I keep my horse in the corral, even when I discover that the horse is sprouting wings. I cannot share symbols if I am galloping around by myself.

Religion gives meaning to life: In former times, among the Saami people of Lappland, when there was need for divination, the shaman consulted his drum. (Yes, his.) Striking the drum caused the markers to jump around on the drum's head, and when the sacred song was completed, the shaman interpreted from the final position of the markers the meaning of life. For on the drum was painted a diagram of the world, symbols of divine spirits and of human destinies, and in the center of the diagram was a stylized tree of life, holding together the universe. The shaman's drum offered meaning by presenting to the people their connection to the life of the rest of the world.

As usual, tradition reserved the drum for men. When at a conference in Australia, to call the group back together after a break, I pretended to sound a didgeridoo, a nun quickly stopped me: only men are supposed to blow the didgeridoo. Once again, the primary symbol system, with its power to interpret our sorrows and joys, is guarded by the males. It's the old story: we women might receive a message, but never give one. Well, we have served notice: at least in Christianity, the didgeridoo orchestra is now co-ed. We women were first at the tomb, and we will describe the Spirit in our midst. We will speak of our feminist Christian faith when we are at home and when we are away, when we lie down and when we rise, our tree of life like a mezuzah on the doorposts of our days.

But I never underestimate the difficulty in contemplating and articulating the meaning of life. How many centuries will it take us to rethink the Christian faith and reshape the Christian community? I think of all those nineteenth-century statues of Mary, forever young, pious, sweet. But on the campus where I teach is a contemporary casting of Mary, Elizabeth Frink's "Walking Madonna." Bronze, slightly larger than life, her bones showing through her meager dress, Mary as an old woman strides across the lawn. You'd better get out of her way; she isn't sitting around praying. And Hadewijch, a thirteenth-century Beguine, wrote of one of her visions: "The angel led me farther, into the center of the space where we were walking. There stood a tree with its roots upward and its summit downward. . . . The angel said to me, 'O mistress, you climb this tree from the beginning to the end, all the way to the profound roots of the incomprehensible God'."[29]

Hadewijch climbing up to the roots, Mary walking resolutely: at least in our search for life together we are not alone.

Religion faces death: Of T. S. Eliot's conversion to Christian faith and practice, Virginia Woolf wrote, "Poor dear Tom Eliot has become an Anglo-Catholic, believes in God and immortality, and goes to church. I was really shocked. A corpse would seem to me more credible than he is. I mean, there's something obscene in a living person sitting by the fire and believing in God."[30]

(A moment of silence to take this in.)

So if Virginia Woolf judged religious observance to be obscene, what does she offer in its place? In her masterpiece *Mrs. Dalloway*, it is a party with which Clarissa tries to reassemble the fragments of post-war London society. Mrs. Dalloway hopes that her perfect party, which even the Prime Minister attends, will glue the pieces together. To do so it must keep out death. Yet one guest, the eminent doctor who sees shellshocked veterans, talks of the day's suicide, and Clarissa thinks, "What business had the Bradshaws to talk of death at her party?"[31] It was almost, one might say, obscene.

Here I must disagree with my magistra Woolf. Our rituals of order, our systems of symbols, the dances at our parties or during our liturgies, these must let death enter in. Like the woman at the well giving water to Jesus, the church receives the other, hoping to embrace the other, the other that is already part of me, the other that I reach toward, as well as the other that I wish to avoid, the other that I haven't even thought about yet, the ultimate other of death. So of the two, a successful party or a renewed Christian worship service, I'll choose the second. It's more about the other, and so it's also more about me.

Any religion worth its salt has to be able to deal with death, not by avoiding it, but by readying for it. If the ritual is Christian, it will remember the dead, it will pray for the dying, it will contemplate the cross. Even the triune God, by including Christ, contains human death; so should also the spirit of our community. But never morbidly: Christianity deals with death by offering it one last meal, one more bite of fresh bread, one more gulp of good wine—the person ministering and the person dying both holding onto a precious gleaming goblet as round as life itself.

We've climbed and climbed, holding hands with one another, passing around the water bottle, bandaging each other's sprains and cuts, and here we are, our treehouse resting in the verdant life of God. And my hope is that, short of breath and exhausted from the climb, we will be amazed to discover that, like Hadewijch, we are not in the branches but in the roots. We thought we were ascending, but in fact we have climbed down, down, down into God. Just as the imagery of the resurrection of the body tried to convey to us, life from God will be other than how we thought life would be. Augustine, I'm sure you know this: it will be other. My dear women co-religionists around the world, it will be other—other than even we imagine. Our life from God, our living in God, will be both cross and tree, both men and women, clods of dirt and colonies of bugs alongside the twelve different fruits that are perpetually ripe, immeasurably juicy, continuously shared.

Endnotes and Book List

1. Virginia Woolf, *The Years* (London: Hogarth Press, 1937), p. 166.
2. C.G. Jung, *Memories, Dreams, Reflections*, ed. Aniela Jaffe, tr. Richard and Clara Winston, rev. ed. (New York: Pantheon Books, 1965), pp. x and viii.
3. *The Life of Christina of Markyate, A Twelfth Century Recluse*, ed. and tr. C.H. Talbot (Oxford: Clarendon Press, 1959), p. 53.
4. Hélène Cixous, *The Hélène Cixous Reader*, ed. Susan Sellers (New York: Routledge, 1994), p. 8. Also see "The Newly Born Woman," pp. 37–45.
5. W.B. Yeats, "Sailing to Byzantium," *The Poems*, Vol. I of *Collected Works of W.B. Yeats*, rev. ed., ed. Richard J. Finneran (New York: Macmillan, 1983), p. 193.
6. Edward Deming Andrews and Faith Andrews, *Visions of the Heavenly Sphere: A Study in Shaker Religious Art* (Charlottesville: University Press of Virginia, 1969), p. 16.
7. Libanius, cited in Wayne A. Meeks, *The First Urban Christians: The Social World of the Apostle Paul* (New Haven: Yale University Press, 1983), p. 214.
8. T.S. Eliot, *The Complete Poems and Plays 1909–1950* (New York: Harcourt, Brace & World, 1958), p. 3.
9. Augustine, "Sermon 52," *Patrologia Latina*, ed. J.P. Migne, Vol. 38 (Paris: 1841), p. 360.
10. Cixous, p. 99.
11. Julian of Norwich, *A Revelation of Love*, ed. Marion Glasscoe, Exeter Medieval English Tests and Studies (Exeter: University of Exeter, 1976), p. 39.
12. Julian, p. 32.
13. Mechthild of Magdeburg, *The Flowing Light of the Godhead*, ed. and tr. Frank Tobin (New York: Paulist Press, 1998), pp. 43–44.
14. Charlotte Bronte, *The Letters of Charlotte Bronte*, ed. Margaret Smith, Vol. I (Oxford: Clarendon Press, 1995), p. 482.
15. *Hadewijch: The Complete Works*, tr. Mother Columba Hart, O.S.B. (New York: Paulist Press, 1980), p. 281.
16. John Updike, "Seven Stanzas at Easter," *Collected Poems, 1953–1993* (New York: Alfred A. Knopf, 1993), pp. 20–21.
17. Walt Whitman, "Song of Myself," *Leaves of Grass*, ed. Harold W. Blodgett and Sculley Bradley (New York: New York University Press, 1965), p. 34.
18. Pseudo-Dionysius Areopagite, "The Mystical Theology," *The Divine Names and Mystical Theology*, tr. John D. James (Milwaukee: Marquette University Press, 1980), p. 221.

19. Catherine of Siena, *The Dialogue*, tr. Suzanne Noffke, O.P. (New York: Paulist Press, 1980), p. 325.
20. Venantius Fortunatus, "The Life of the Holy Radegund," *The Sainted Women of the Dark Ages*, ed. and tr. Jo Ann McNamara and John E. Halborg (Durham: Duke University Press, 1992), p. 70.
21. *The Book of Margery Kempe*, tr. B.A. Windeatt (New York: Penguin, 1985), p. 104.
22. *The Martin Luther Christmas Book*, tr. and ed. Roland H. Bainton (Philadelphia: Muhlenberg Press, 1948), p. 38.
23. Augustine, *The Confessions of St. Augustine*, tr. John K. Ryan (New York: Image Doubleday, 1960), p. 44.
24. Augustine, p. 93.
25. *1001 Questions and Answers on the Christian Life* (LaGrange, IN: Pathway Publishers, 1992), pp. 74–75.
26. Elizabeth A. Johnson, *She Who Is: The Mystery of God in Feminist Theological Discourse* (New York: Crossroad, 1992), p. 235.
27. Larry L. Rasmussen, *Earth Community, Earth Ethics* (Geneva: WCC Publications, 1996), p. 275.
28. Annie Dillard, *Holy the Firm* (New York: Harper & Row, 1977), p. 59.
29. *Hadewijch: The Complete Works*, p. 266.
30. Virginia Woolf, *The Letters of Virginia Woolf*, ed. Nigel Nicolson and Joanne Trautmann, Vol. III (New York: Harcourt Brace Jovanovich, 1977), pp. 457–58.
31. Virginia Woolf, *Mrs. Dalloway* (New York: Harcourt Brace & Company, 1925), p. 280.

Some Other Books I've Read

Bynum, Caroline Walker. *Holy Feast and Holy Fast: The Religious Significance of Food to Medieval Women*. Berkeley: University of California Press, 1987.

Cook, Roger. *The Tree of Life: Image for the Cosmos*. New York: Thames and Hudson, 1988.

Donovan, Josephine. *Feminist Theory: The Intellectual Traditions of American Feminism*. New expanded edition. New York: Continuum, 1997.

Frymer-Kensky, Tikva. *In the Wake of the Goddesses: Women, Culture and the Biblical Transformation of Pagan Myth*. New York: Fawcett Columbine, 1992.

Haskins, Susan. *Mary Magdalen: Myth and Metaphor*. London: HarperColllins, 1993.

Henry, Avril, ed. *Biblia Pauperum: A Facsimile of the Forty-Page Blockbook*. Ithaca, New York: Cornell University Press, 1987.

Jung, Carl G. *Man and His Symbols*. New York: Doubleday and Company, 1964.

Kraybill, Donald B. *The Riddle of Amish Culture*. Baltimore: Johns Hopkins University Press, 1989.

LaCugna, Catherine Mowry. *God for Us: The Trinity and Christian Life*. San Francisco: HarperCollins, 1991.

Langer, Susanne K. *Philosophy in a New Key: A Study in the Symbolism of Reason, Rite, and Art.* Cambridge: Harvard University Press, 1942.

Lerner, Gerda. *The Creation of Feminist Consciousness: From the Middle Ages to Eighteen-seventy.* New York: Oxford University Press, 1993.

Lerner, Gerda. *The Creation of Patriarchy.* New York: Oxford University Press, 1986.

McDonnell, Colleen, and Lang, Bernhard. *Heaven: A History.* New Haven: Yale University Press, 1988.

McFague, Sallie. *The Body of God: An Ecological Theology.* Minneapolis: Fortress Press, 1993.

Petroff, Elizabeth Alvilda. *Medieval Women's Visionary Literature.* New York: Oxford University Press, 1986.

Poole, Stafford. *Our Lady of Guadalupe: The Origins and Sources of a Mexican National Symbol, 1531–1797.* Tuscon: University of Arizona Press, 1995.

Power, Kim. *Veiled Desire: Augustine on Women.* New York: Continuum, 1996.

Ricoeur, Paul. *The Rule of Metaphor: Multi-disciplinary Studies of the Creation of Meaning in Language.* Translated from the French by Robert Czerny. Toronto: University of Toronto Press, 1977.

Ruether, Rosemary Radford. *Sexism and God-Talk: Toward a Feminist Theology.* 10th anniversary edition. Boston: Beacon Press, 1993.

Starhawk. *The Spiral Dance: A Rebirth of the Ancient Religion of the Great Goddess.* Revised edition. San Francisco: Harper, 1989.

Stein, Stephen J. *The Shaker Experience in America: A History of the United Society of Believers.* New Haven: Yale University Press, 1992.

Wilder, Amos Niven. *Theopoetic: Theology and the Religious Imagination.* Philadelphia: Fortress Press, 1976.

Woolf, Virginia. *A Room of One's Own.* New York: Harcourt Brace Jovanovich, 1929.